GLUTEN-FREE
COOK BOOK

GLUTEN-FREE
COOK BOOK

k

Published by
Kandour Ltd
1-3 Colebrooke Place
London N1 8HZ

This edition published 2005

This edition printed in 2005 for
Bookmart Ltd
Registered Number 2372865
Trading As Bookmart Ltd
Blaby Road
Wigston
Leicester
LE18 4SE

Title: Gluten-Free Cook Book

Editorial and design management: Metro Media
Author: Victoria Worsley
Design/layout: Lee Coventry
Original design concept: Christine Fent
Photography: photos.com

Printed and bound in India

ISBN 1-904756-31-X

CONTENTS

CONTENTS

INTRODUCTION

Gluten is a protein that can be found in many cereal grains. In some people it can trigger a severe reaction – these people are said to be suffering from coeliac disease. Some people also find they react badly to gluten, although not as strongly. This is known as having a gluten intolerance. Always seek expert medical advice if you believe you have a food allergy or intolerance, and before embarking on a gluten-free diet.

However, once a gluten-free diet is recommended, it can be easy to think that there is not much interesting food to eat. This cookbook dispels that idea, providing you with recipes that are tasty, varied and interesting, as well as being gluten-free. So whether you yourself are gluten intolerant, or you are cooking for friends and family who suffer from coeliac disease, there are plenty of ideas here.

As bread and cakes are some of the main things that are banned under a gluten-free diet, we have included here a section for gluten-free breads and another for gluten-free cakes – to prove that going without gluten does not mean missing out on treats!

SOUPS

Whether as a starter, a snack or a light lunch, nothing beats a warm bowl of soup in the winter. However, canned or packet soup rarely has the texture and rich flavour of home-made broths, so here is a collection of nourishing and healthy soups for you and your family to enjoy – with no more scouring the lists of ingredients and worrying about gluten. You'll find classic flavours such as carrot, pea, black bean and leek and potato. Both vegetarians and meat-eaters are catered for. And if you're cooking for a larger number of guests, just increase the ingredients accordingly!

SOUPS

CARROT SOUP

Serves 4

INGREDIENTS
100g/4oz onions, finely chopped
100g/4oz swede, finely chopped
275g/10oz carrot, grated
25g/1oz butter
Salt and pepper
600ml/1pt vegetable stock
150ml/^{1}/$_4$pt milk

In a large saucepan cook the onions, 225g/8oz carrots and swede in the butter for 10 minutes and season well.

Add the stock and bring to the boil. Lower the heat and simmer gently for 40 minutes. Allow to cool slightly, then purée in a blender or food processor until smooth. Bring back to the boil, stir in the milk and serve garnished with the remaining carrot.

LEEK AND POTATO SOUP

Serves 4

INGREDIENTS
25g/1oz butter
100g/4oz onions, finely chopped
100g/4oz leeks, chopped
600ml/1pt vegetable stock
225g/8oz potatoes, finely chopped
Salt and pepper
2 tbsp chopped fresh chives

In a large saucepan, melt the butter and cook the onions and leeks gently for 10 minutes. Add stock, potatoes and seasoning. Bring to the boil, then reduce the heat and simmer gently for 40 minutes.

Allow to cool slightly and then purée in a blender or food processor. Bring back to the boil before serving garnished with the chives.

CHICKEN AND HAM SOUP

Serves 8

INGREDIENTS
2 tbsp olive oil
4 chicken thighs, skinned
2 celery sticks, sliced
3 onions, chopped
350g/12oz gammon, cut into 1cm/1/2in chunks
2 bay leaves
600ml/1pt chicken stock
600ml/1pt water
300g/11oz potatoes, diced
150g/5oz canned sweetcorn, drained

Heat the oil in a large, heavy-based saucepan. Add the chicken, celery and onions, and fry gently for 10 minutes, stirring until golden.

Add the gammon, bay leaves, stock and water and bring to the boil. Reduce the heat, cover and simmer gently for 40 minutes until the meat is tender.

Remove the chicken and shred the flesh from the bones, then return to the pan and add the potatoes and sweetcorn. Simmer, covered, for 20 minutes, until the potatoes are tender. Serve hot.

VEGETABLE AND RICE SOUP

Serves 6

INGREDIENTS

200g/7oz cabbage, chopped
2 celery stalks, chopped
3 carrots, sliced
1 onion, chopped
50g/2oz fresh parsley, chopped
2 cloves garlic, crushed
3 tbsp vegetable oil
900ml/1 1/2pts vegetable stock
450g/1lb canned stewed tomatoes
275g/10oz canned sweetcorn
150g/5oz long grain rice
Salt and pepper
450g/1lb canned red kidney beans

In a large pot, over a medium heat, sauté the cabbage, celery, carrots, onion, parsley and garlic in the oil for about 5 minutes. Add the stock, tomatoes, sweetcorn, rice and seasoning, then bring to boil and simmer, stirring occasionally for 10 minutes.

Reduce the heat and stir in the kidney beans. Simmer for a further 1 hour, then season to taste before serving.

POTATO AND SPINACH SOUP

Serves 6

INGREDIENTS
900g/2lb potatoes, diced
2 celery sticks, chopped
1 onion, finely chopped
1 garlic clove, crushed
1.2 litres/2pts vegetable stock
Salt and pepper
200g/7oz fresh spinach leaves
250g/9oz low-fat cream cheese
300ml/1/2pt milk
Salt and pepper
1 tsp dry sherry

Place the potatoes, celery, onion and garlic in a large saucepan. Add the stock and simmer for 20 minutes.

Season the soup, add the spinach, then cook for a further 10 minutes. Remove from the heat and allow to cool slightly.

Process the soup in batches in a blender or food processor until smooth and return to the saucepan. Stir in the cream cheese and milk, then simmer gently until warmed through. Check the seasoning and add the sherry before serving.

GINGER, PUMPKIN AND COCONUT SOUP

Serves 8

INGREDIENTS

1 onion, chopped
3 garlic cloves, crushed
2 tbsp olive oil
1 medium pumpkin, cut into bite-size pieces
600ml/1pt vegetable stock
2 tbsp grated fresh ginger
300ml/^{1}/$_2$pt coconut cream
Salt and pepper

Heat the oil in a large frying pan and sauté the onion and garlic until golden. Add the pumpkin and sauté, stirring, for 5 minutes. Add enough stock to cover the pumpkin, then add the ginger.

Bring to the boil and simmer for 15 minutes, or until the pumpkin is soft. Remove from the heat and allow to cool, then blend the mixture to a purée in a blender or food processor.

Return to the heat, add the coconut cream and season to taste. Bring the heat up slowly until the soup is simmering. Adjust seasoning to taste before serving.

PEA SOUP

Serves 4

INGREDIENTS

175g/6oz dried whole peas
1.2 litres/2pts vegetable stock
1 large onion, finely chopped
2 celery stalks, finely chopped
1/2 tsp dried sage
1/4 tsp dried thyme
Salt and pepper
1 tsp dried parsley

Soak the peas in plenty of water overnight, then drain and rinse.

In a large saucepan cover the peas with the stock, bring to the boil, then reduce the heat, cover and simmer gently for 1 to 1½ hours until soft. You may need to add water if the stock evaporates too quickly.

Add the onion and celery to the soup along with the sage, thyme, seasoning and parsley.

Bring to the boil and cook the soup for a further 15 minutes. Blend in a blender or food processor until smooth, then reheat gently and serve hot.

CLAM SOUP

Serves 6

INGREDIENTS
1.2 litres/2pts water
1 large onion, very finely chopped
1.2 litres/2pts fish stock
2 garlic cloves, crushed
150ml/¼pt white wine
2 bay leaves
200g/7oz tuna fish in brine, drained
900g/2lb fresh clams
¼ tsp gluten-free chilli sauce
2 tbsp chopped fresh parsley

Put the water and onion into a large pan over a high heat, cover with a lid and bring it to the boil. Cook for 5 minutes and then drain away the water. Return the onions to the pan and cover them with the same amount of fresh water. Add the stock and cook over a medium heat for 10 minutes.

Add the garlic, wine and bay leaves and simmer for a further 10 minutes. Reduce the heat and simmer until the onions are soft and the liquid has reduced by half.

Mix in the tuna, clams, chilli sauce and half the parsley and simmer gently without boiling until the clams are heated through. Serve the soup immediately, sprinkled with the remaining parsley.

CABBAGE SOUP

Serves 6

INGREDIENTS
1 tbsp olive oil
450g/1lb minced beef
1 onion, chopped
100g/4oz celery, diced
1/2 green pepper
Salt and pepper
1/2 tsp paprika
800g/1lb 12oz canned chopped tomatoes
600ml/1pt vegetable stock
2 red chillies, seeded and chopped
3 tbsp chopped fresh parsley
200g/7oz potatoes, cubed
150g/5oz carrots, diced
200g/7oz green cabbage, chopped

Heat the oil in a large saucepan, then add the beef and cook until browned. Add the onion, celery and green pepper and sauté for a further 5 minutes.

Add seasoning, paprika, tomatoes, stock, chillies, parsley, potatoes and carrots and cook, uncovered, for 1 hour.

Add the cabbage and cook for a further 1 hour. Adjust the seasoning to taste and serve hot.

BLACK BEAN SOUP

Serves 6

INGREDIENTS
300g/11oz dried black beans
2 red chillies, seeded and chopped
1 large onion, chopped
3 tbsp olive oil
1 garlic clove, crushed
2 litres/3pts vegetable stock
2 carrots, sliced
2 celery sticks, sliced
2 sprigs of thyme
1 bay leaf
1 tsp ground cloves
Salt and pepper

Soak the black beans in water overnight, then drain well and reserve.

In a large pan, cook the chillies and onion in the oil for 5 minutes until soft. Add the beans and garlic, then pour in the stock.

Add the carrots, celery, thyme, bay leaf and cloves. Season to taste and simmer for $1^1/_2$ hours, or until the beans are soft. Top up with water if necessary.

Leave the soup to cool, then remove the bay leaf and transfer the mixture to a blender or food processor and purée until smooth. Adjust the seasoning and reheat gently. Serve hot.

STARTERS
&
SALADS

Everyone wants their dinner parties to go down well, and what better way to begin than with a great starter? Just because you're cooking for someone who's gluten-intolerant, there is no reason to skip this course. There is a wide variety in this section — from deep-fried foods to healthy dips, from fruit salads to light omelettes, there should be something to suit every taste and occasion. Many of these dishes would also make great snacks, or even — in the case of deep-fried mushrooms — fantastic finger food to be passed around at parties.

AUBERGINE SALAD

Serves 4

INGREDIENTS
2 aubergines, sliced
75ml/3fl oz olive oil
2 garlic cloves, crushed
1 tbsp lemon juice
50ml/2fl oz red wine vinegar
1/2 tsp ground coriander
1/2 tsp ground cumin
Salt and pepper
1/2 cucumber, thinly sliced
2 tomatoes, thinly sliced
2 tbsp natural yogurt, to serve

Brush the aubergine slices lightly with 1 tablespoon oil and cook under a hot grill, turning once, until golden. Cut the cooked aubergine slices into quarters.

Mix together the remaining oil with the garlic, lemon juice, vinegar, coriander and cumin. Season to taste and mix thoroughly. Add the aubergines, stir well and chill in the refrigerator for at least 2 hours.

Add the cucumber and tomatoes and mix well. Transfer to a serving dish and spoon the yogurt on top to serve.

PINK GRAPEFRUIT SALAD

Serves 8

INGREDIENTS
2 garlic cloves, crushed
250g/9oz parsley, trimmed and chopped
1 tsp balsamic vinegar
2 tbsp olive oil
Salt and pepper
10cm/4in fresh ginger, peeled
6 large pink grapefruit, peeled
50g/2oz lamb's lettuce

Make the dressing in a large bowl by beating together the garlic, parsley, vinegar, oil and seasoning. Grate in all of the ginger.

Segment the grapefruit, removing all pith, skin and pips, and toss in the dressing. Leave to marinate covered in the refrigerator, for 3 hours. Line a salad bowl with the lamb's lettuce and spoon the grapefruit and dressing on top to serve.

DEEP-FRIED MUSHROOMS

Serves 4

INGREDIENTS
50g/2oz apple, grated
1 egg
2 tbsp milk
25g/1oz gram flour
25g/1oz rice flour
Pinch of salt
1/4 tsp bicarbonate of soda
1/4 tsp cream of tartar
225g/8oz button mushrooms
Vegetable oil, for deep-frying

In a blender or food processor, purée the apple, egg and milk.

In a large bowl mix together the gram flour, rice flour, salt, bicarbonate of soda and cream of tartar Fold the purée and dry mixture together to make a sticky batter.

In a large pan, heat the oil to 190°C/375°F or until a cube of bread browns in 30 seconds.

Dip the mushrooms individually in the batter to coat them and then lower them into the oil. Fry until golden brown. Drain on kitchen paper before serving.

PEA AND POTATO SALAD

Serves 6

INGREDIENTS
900g/2lb red potatoes, chopped into bite-size pieces
200g/7oz frozen peas
75g/3oz mayonnaise
1 tbsp Dijon mustard
1 tbsp apple cider vinegar
1 tsp dried tarragon
1/2 tsp salt
150g/5oz red onions, finely chopped

In a large saucepan bring the potatoes to a boil in lightly salted water. Reduce the heat and simmer for about 20 to 25 minutes, until tender.

Just before the potatoes are done, add the peas and cook for a further 2 minutes, then drain and leave to cool to room temperature.

In a large bowl, combine the mayonnaise, mustard, vinegar, tarragon and salt. Add the potatoes, peas and onion and stir well until coated. Chill in the refrigerator for 1 hour before serving.

CARROT AND APRICOT PATE

Serves 6

INGREDIENTS
Butter, for greasing
75g/3oz dried apricots, finely chopped
125ml/4fl oz water
75g/3oz tofu, grated
Salt and pepper
1 tbsp lemon juice
25g/1oz ground almonds
1/3 tsp cardamom
225g/8oz carrot, grated

Preheat the oven to 200°C/400°F/Gas mark 6. Lightly grease a
small loaf tin with butter.

Place the apricots in a saucepan and cover with the water.
Simmer for 10 minutes.

Mix together the tofu, seasoning, lemon juice, almonds,
cardamom and carrots in a large bowl. Add the apricots and any
remaining cooking liquid and mix well.

Place in the loaf tin and bake for 45 minutes. Allow to cool
slightly before serving.

SMOKED SALMON SPREAD

Serves 4

INGREDIENTS
225g/8oz smoked salmon
225g/8oz cream cheese
1 tbsp lemon juice
2 tbsp mashed gluten-free capers
Dash Tabasco sauce
100g/4oz red onion, finely chopped

Blend the salmon, cream cheese and lemon juice in a blender or food processor until smooth, then stir in the capers and Tabasco sauce.

Season to taste, then stir in the onion and chill in the refrigerator for several hours before serving.

HUMMUS

Serves 6

INGREDIENTS
150g/5oz dried chickpeas
Juice of 2 lemons
2 tbsp olive oil
2 garlic cloves, sliced
1/4 tsp cayenne pepper
150ml/1/4pt tahini paste
Salt and pepper

Put the chickpeas in a bowl, cover with plenty of cold water and leave to soak overnight.

Drain the chickpeas and cover with fresh water in a saucepan. Bring to the boil and boil rapidly for about 10 minutes. Reduce the heat and simmer gently for about 2 hours until soft. Drain.

Drain the chickpeas, then process in a blender or food processor to a smooth purée. Add the lemon juice, olive oil, garlic, cayenne pepper and tahini and blend until creamy.

Season the purée with salt and pepper and transfer to a serving dish. Sprinkle with oil and cayenne pepper and serve with olives.

BROAD BEAN DIP

Serves 6

INGREDIENTS
100g/4oz dried broad beans
2 garlic cloves, peeled
1 tsp cumin seeds
50ml/2fl oz olive oil
Salt and pepper
Mint sprigs, to garnish
Extra cumin seeds, cayenne pepper and vegetable crudités to serve

Place the broad beans in a bowl, cover with cold water and leave to soak overnight. Drain thoroughly.

Place the beans in a pan with the garlic and cumin seeds and enough water just to cover. Bring to the boil, then reduce the heat and simmer until the beans are tender. Drain and cool, then remove the outer skin of each bean.

Purée the beans in a blender or food processor, adding the oil and enough water to give a smooth dip. Season with salt and pepper. Garnish with sprigs of mint, cumin and cayenne pepper and serve with crudités.

BACON AND MUSHROOM APPETIZERS

Serves 4

INGREDIENTS
225g/8oz mushrooms
150ml/¼pt Italian dressing
6 slices back bacon

Marinate the mushrooms in the Italian dressing for 6 hours.

Cut the bacon into pieces that will fit each mushroom, then wrap
bacon around each mushroom and secure with a cocktail stick.

Grill under a medium heat, until the bacon is cooked and the
mushrooms are tender. This should take about 8 minutes,
depending on the size of mushrooms.

ORANGE AND TOMATO SALAD

Serves 4

INGREDIENTS
4 beef tomatoes, sliced
225g/8oz goats' cheese, cut into 4 thick rounds
2 oranges, peeled and sliced
50g/2oz chopped chives

Arrange the tomato slices in a circle on serving places, then top
with a circle of cheese slabs, then a smaller circle of oranges.
Serve scattered with chives.

MEAT MAINS

When you're suffering from a food intolerance, it is easy to be bogged down and intimidated by the long list of foods you have to avoid. You may often find yourself eating the same dish over and over again, simply because you know it is safe. This section will change all that as here is a wide selection of meat dishes – all gluten-free – to suit all tastes. From roasts to burgers, and with inspiration coming from across the globe, you need never find yourself stuck in an eating rut again.

PARMA HAM STUFFED PORK

Serves 4

INGREDIENTS

500g/1lb 2oz lean pork fillet, trimmed
Salt and pepper
Small bunch fresh basil leaves
2 tbsp grated Parmesan cheese
2 tbsp sun-dried tomato paste
6 thin slices Parma ham
1 tbsp olive oil

Preheat the oven to 190°C/375°F/Gas mark 5.

Slice the pork fillet lengthways down the middle, taking care not to cut all the way through. Open out the pork and season well, then lay the basil leaves down the centre.

Mix the Parmesan and tomato paste and spread the mixture over the basil, then press the pork back together.

Wrap the Parma ham around the pork, overlapping to cover. Place on a rack in a roasting tin seamside down and brush with oil. Bake in the oven for 30 to 40 minutes until cooked through. Allow to stand for 10 minutes. Drain the pork and slice thinly to serve.

BEEF WITH HORSERADISH

Serves 4

INGREDIENTS
4 beef steaks, cubed
1 onion, chopped
2 tbsp butter
2 tbsp gluten-free soy sauce
125ml/4fl oz white wine
Salt and pepper
200ml/7fl oz sour cream
2 tsp prepared horseradish
2 tsp chopped fresh dill

Brown the steaks and onion lightly in the butter in a frying pan over a medium heat. Add the soy sauce and wine and season to taste. Cover and simmer 35 to 40 minutes, or until tender.

In a small bowl, combine the sour cream, horseradish and dill, then stir into the steak mixture and heat through for about 4 minutes before serving.

CHICKEN WITH SWEET ONION RELISH

Serves 4

INGREDIENTS
2 tsp olive oil
450g/1lb sweet onions, diced
1/2 tsp black pepper
4 chicken thighs, about 175g/6oz each, skinned
1/4 tsp dried oregano
1/2 tsp dried thyme
5 tsp balsamic vinegar
1 tbsp chopped fresh parsley

Heat the oil in a large frying pan over a medium heat and sauté the onions with half the pepper for about 5 minutes, until the onions are soft and golden.

Add the remaining pepper, to the pan with the chicken, oregano, and thyme, and sprinkle with 4 teaspoons balsamic vinegar.

Cover, reduce the heat, and simmer for 25 minutes or until the chicken is cooked. Uncover, increase the heat and cook for 2 minutes or until the liquid almost evaporates.

Stir in the remaining vinegar and sprinkle with the parsley.

TURKEY MARSALA

Serves 4

INGREDIENTS
6 slices cooked turkey breast
1 egg, lightly beaten
100g/4oz cornflour
50g/2oz butter
Salt and pepper
2 tbsp olive oil
225g/8oz mushrooms
125ml/4fl oz chicken stock
50ml/2fl oz Marsala
100g/4oz Mozzarella cheese, grated

Preheat the oven to 180°C/350°F/Gas mark 4.

Dip turkey slices in the egg, then the cornflour. In a frying pan, sauté the turkey in half the butter and season to taste. Place the cooked meat in a large baking dish. Add 1 tablespoon oil to the pan and sauté the mushrooms.

Mix the stock and Marsala and pour over the turkey in the baking dish. Sprinkle the Mozzarella and the mushrooms over the turkey and cook in the oven for 20 minutes, until the cheese melts.

CHINESE-STYLE PORK

Serves 4

INGREDIENTS
1 red onion, peeled and finely chopped
300ml/¹/₂pt water
300ml/¹/₂pt gluten-free vegetable stock
300ml/¹/₂pt unsweetened pineapple juice
Salt and pepper
2 tbsp tomato ketchup
2 small carrots, peeled and cut into matchsticks
1 red pepper, cored and thinly sliced
1 yellow pepper, cored and thinly sliced
1 red chilli, seeded and thinly sliced
2 garlic cloves, peeled and crushed
1 tbsp grated fresh ginger
400g/14oz stir-fry lean pork pieces, all fat removed
300g/11oz mangetouts, trimmed
2 tbsp gluten-free soy sauce
1 tbsp cornflour
1 tbsp white wine vinegar
Chopped fresh coriander leaves, to garnish

Put the onion and water in a non-stick frying pan or wok, and bring to the boil over a high heat. Cook the onion until the water has evaporated, then add the stock and pineapple juice. Season with salt and pepper, stir in the ketchup and add the carrots, peppers, chilli, garlic and ginger. Cook for 5 minutes, then add the pork, mangetouts and soy sauce. Cook for 3 to 4 minutes, stirring the ingredients frequently to make sure that they are evenly cooked and coated with the sauce.

Mix the cornflour and vinegar together. Stir this into the mixture and cook until the sauce is thick, clear and coating all the ingredients.

Sprinkle with chopped fresh coriander leaves and serve immediately with boiled rice noodles.

CHICKEN CASSEROLE

Serves 4

INGREDIENTS
1 garlic clove, crushed
50g/2oz mushrooms, halved
1 onion, chopped
1 celery stalk, chopped
1/4 green pepper, chopped
2 carrots, chopped
300ml/1/2pt water
1 tbsp tomato purée
1/2 tsp paprika
1 bay leaf
1/2 tsp dried marjoram
1/2 tsp dried rosemary
1/4 tsp dried sage
Salt and pepper
4 chicken joints, skinned
1 tsp cornflour

Preheat the oven to 200°C/400°F/Gas mark 6.

Place the garlic, mushrooms, onion, celery, green pepper and carrots in a casserole dish.

Mix together the water, tomato purée, paprika, bay leaf, marjoram, rosemary, sage and seasoning and pour over the vegetables.

Add the chicken pieces, cover the casserole dish and cook in the oven for 1 1/4 hours or until the chicken is tender.

Stir the cornflour in 2 teaspoons water and add to the casserole. Reheat, remove the bay leaf and serve with rice.

PORK WITH CHERRY SAUCE

Serves 4

INGREDIENTS
8 pork chops
300g/11oz glace cherries, halved
75ml/3fl oz golden syrup
50g/2oz slivered almonds
75ml/3fl oz red wine vinegar
$1/4$ tsp salt
$1/8$ tsp black pepper
$1/4$ tsp grated nutmeg
$1/4$ tsp ground cloves
$1/4$ tsp cinnamon

In a large saucepan, combine the cherries, golden syrup, vinegar, salt, pepper and spices. Bring to boil and boil for 1 minute, then add the almonds.

Fry the pork chops in a frying pan until cooked through. Pour a third of the sauce over the frying chops. Pour the remaining sauce over the chops when serving.

SWEET AND SOUR MEATBALLS

Serves 4

INGREDIENTS
675g/1$1/2$lb lean minced beef
75g/3oz onion soup mix
50g/2oz gluten-free breadcrumbs
2 eggs, beaten
50g/2oz butter
275g/10oz grape jam
125ml/4fl oz chilli sauce

Add the beef, soup mix and breadcrumbs to the egg, and beat until the mixture forms the right consistency to form balls.

Fry the balls in a frying pan in the butter until browned all over. In a separate saucepan, mix the jam and chilli sauce. Add meatballs to the sauce and heat over a medium heat for about 30 to 45 minutes. Serve warm.

CHICKEN AND PESTO PASTA

Serves 6

INGREDIENTS
300ml/^{1}/$_2$pt olive oil
3 fresh rosemary sprigs
4 chicken breasts
500g/1lb 2oz gluten-free rice pasta tubes
50g/2oz fresh coriander
25g/1oz fresh parsley
1 garlic clove, peeled and crushed
100g/4oz pine nuts, ground
Salt and pepper

Brush a grill pan with a little of the oil. Place the rosemary and chicken breasts in the pan and cook for about 10 minutes, until the chicken is cooked through. Discard the skin, then slice the chicken into bite-size pieces. Discard the rosemary.

Boil the pasta in a pan of lightly salted water until al dente, then drain. Toss in a bowl with 1 tablespoon olive oil. Mix in the chicken pieces.

In a blender or food processor, blend the remaining oil with the coriander, parsley, garlic and pine nuts until smooth. Stir the coriander sauce into the pasta and serve immediately.

COTTAGE PIE

Serves 4

INGREDIENTS
4 potatoes, chopped
4 carrots, chopped
1 swede, chopped
1 tbsp olive oil
1 onion, chopped
450g/1lb minced beef
400g/14oz canned chopped tomatoes
2 garlic cloves, crushed

Preheat the oven to 200°C/400°F/Gas mark 6.

Cook the potatoes in boiling water until soft, then drain and mash.
Cook the carrot and swede together in boiling water, then mash.

Heat the oil in a pan and cook the onion for 3 minutes. Add the
minced beef to the frying pan and cook for 8 minutes over a
medium heat, stirring occasionally.

Add the tomatoes and garlic to the minced beef and bring to a
simmer. Transfer the beef and tomato to a casserole dish. Layer
the swede and carrot above the beef and top with the potato.

Bake in the oven for 20 minutes.

BEEF STIR-FRY

Serves 4

INGREDIENTS

2 tsp gluten-free cornflour
3 tbsp ruby port
3 tbsp gluten-free soy sauce
1 tbsp sunflower oil
350g/12oz lean beef steak, cut into thin strips
2.5cm/1in piece fresh ginger, peeled and finely chopped
1 garlic clove, crushed
1 red pepper, sliced
225g/8oz broccoli florets
Salt and pepper

Blend the cornflour with the port and soy sauce in a small bowl.

Heat the oil in a large frying pan, add the beef, ginger and garlic
and stir-fry over a medium heat for 3 minutes until the beef is
browned. Add the pepper and broccoli and stir-fry for a further 5
minutes, until the vegetables are tender.

Add the cornflour mixture and seasoning to the pan, then cook,
stirring constantly until the sauce thickens. Lower the heat and
stir-fry for a further 1 minute, then serve at once.

CHEESE, POTATO AND HAM CASSEROLE

Serves 6

INGREDIENTS
3 potatoes, thinly sliced
1 onion, sliced
Salt and pepper
75g/3oz Cheddar cheese, grated
75g/3oz cooked ham, chopped
2 tbsp gluten-free chutney
2 hard-boiled eggs, chopped
125ml/4fl oz milk
1/4 tsp paprika

Preheat the oven to 180°C/350°F/Gas mark 4.

Line an ovenproof dish with half the potato and onion slices, then sprinkle with salt and pepper. Spread the cheese, ham, chutney and eggs over the potato slices.

Use the remaining potato and onion slices to make another layer, then pour the milk over the top and sprinkle with the paprika.

Bake in the oven for about 30 minutes and serve hot.

BEEF TAGINE

Serves 4

INGREDIENTS

2 tbsp sunflower oil
900g/2lb stewing beef, trimmed and cut into 2.5cm/1in cubes
Pinch of ground turmeric
1 red chilli, seeded and chopped
1 large onion, chopped
1½ tsp paprika
½ tsp ground cumin
Pinch of cayenne pepper
1 tbsp chopped fresh parsley
1 tbsp chopped fresh coriander
450g/1lb sweet potatoes, sliced
15g/½oz butter
Salt and pepper

Heat the oil in a flameproof casserole dish and fry the beef and turmeric, over a medium heat for 4 to 5 minutes until browned all over.

Cover the pan and cook for 15 minutes over a low heat, stirring frequently.

Meanwhile, preheat the oven to 180°C/350°F/Gas mark 4.

Add the chilli, onion, paprika, cumin and cayenne pepper to the pan, together with enough water to cover the meat. Cover tightly and cook in the oven for 1 to 1½ hours until the meat is tender, add a little water if necessary to keep the stew moist.

Add the parsley and coriander to the meat and arrange the sweet potato slices over the top, then dot with the butter. Cover and cook in the oven for a further 10 minutes.

Remove the lid of the casserole dish and cook under a hot grill for 5 to 10 minutes until golden.

43

CHICKEN HOTPOT

Serves 4

INGREDIENTS
450g/1lb chicken joints
25g/1oz gram flour
1 tbsp olive oil
100g/4oz onion, chopped
100g/4oz swede, chopped
100g/4oz parsnip, chopped
225g/8oz mushrooms
400g/14oz canned chopped tomatoes
2 garlic cloves, crushed
1 tsp dried mixed herbs
25g/1oz lentils
Salt and pepper
300ml/1/2pt chicken stock or water

Preheat the oven to 190°C/375°F/Gas mark 5.

Remove the skin from the chicken and roll the joints in the flour.

Fry the chicken gently in oil until browned on both sides and then place in a casserole dish.

Fry the onion until translucent and then add to the casserole dish.

Add the swede and parsnip together with the mushrooms, tomatoes, garlic, mixed herbs and lentils. Sprinkle with seasoning and add enough stock to cover.

Cook in the oven for 30 minutes and then lower the oven temperature to 150°C/300°F/Gas mark 2 and cook the casserole for a further 1 hour.

LASAGNE

Serves 8

INGREDIENTS

Vegetable oil, for greasing
450g/1lb minced beef
1 onion, chopped
3 garlic cloves, crushed
900g/2lb canned chopped tomatoes
225g/8oz tomato sauce
175g/6oz tomato purée
4 tbsp chopped fresh parsley
2 tsp dried oregano
1 tsp chopped fresh basil
450g/1lb cottage cheese
100g/4oz Parmesan cheese, grated
1 egg white, beaten
12 gluten-free lasagne sheets

Preheat the oven to 180°C/350°F/Gas mark 4. Lightly grease a 32x23cm/13x9in baking tin with oil.

Cook the meat, onion and garlic in a large frying pan until the meat is browned, stirring well.

In a large saucepan combine the tomatoes, tomato sauce, tomato purée, half of the parsley, the oregano, basil and the meat mixture. Bring to the boil, then simmer for about 20 minutes.

Combine the remaining parsley, cottage cheese, Parmesan and egg white in a bowl and stir well. Cook the lasagne sheets in salted boiling water, according to package directions, and drain well.

Spread a quarter of the tomato mixture in the bottom of the baking tin. Arrange 4 noodles over the top, then top with a third of the cottage cheese mixture. Repeat the layers, ending with the tomato mixture.

Bake, covered, for 50 minutes, then uncovered for a further 10 minutes. Remove from the oven and let stand for 10 minutes before serving.

CHICKEN KEBABS

Serves 4

INGREDIENTS
1 tbsp tomato purée
1 garlic clove, crushed
1/2 tsp ground ginger
1 tsp paprika
2 tbsp olive oil
1 tbsp lemon juice
550g/1lb 4oz skinned chicken, cubed
1 onion, quartered
8 mushrooms (optional)
Parsley to garnish

Preheat the oven to 200°C/400°F/Gas mark 6.

Mix together the tomato purée, garlic, ginger, paprika, oil and lemon juice to form a marinade. Toss the chicken in the marinade and leave to stand for 3 hours.

Separate each onion quarter into its layers. Thread the chicken, mushrooms (optional) and onion layers on to 4 large skewers. Brush the vegetables with the marinade.

Place on a baking tray and bake in the oven for 30 minutes, turning once during cooking.

Serve garnished with chopped parsley.

STOVED CHICKEN

Serves 4

INGREDIENTS

900g/2lb baking potatoes, cut into 5mm/^{1}/$_4$in slices
2 onions, thinly sliced
1 tbsp chopped fresh thyme
Salt and pepper
25g/1oz butter
1 tbsp vegetable oil
3 slices back bacon, chopped
4 large chicken joints, halved
600ml/1pt chicken stock
1 bay leaf

Preheat the oven to 150°C/300°F/Gas mark 2.

Arrange half the potato slices in a layer on the bottom of a large casserole dish, then cover with half the onions. Sprinkle with half of the thyme, and season.

Heat the butter and oil in a large heavy-based frying pan, add the bacon and chicken and brown on all sides. Remove the chicken and shred the flesh, then transfer the chicken and bacon to the casserole dish, reserving the fat in the pan.

Sprinkle the remaining thyme over the casserole dish, season with salt and pepper, then cover with the remaining onions, followed by a layer of potato slices.

Pour the stock over the potatoes. Tuck in the bay leaf and brush the potatoes with the reserved fat. Cover and bake for 1^1/$_2$ hours, or until the chicken is tender.

Preheat the grill. Uncover the casserole dish and grill until the potato is brown and crisp. Remove the bay leaf and serve.

LAMB WITH CELERIAC

Serves 6

INGREDIENTS
For the sauce:
400g/14oz natural soya yogurt
4 tbsp chopped fresh coriander leaves
1 red chilli, seeded and finely chopped
Salt and pepper

750g/1lb 10oz minced lamb
1 onion, chopped
4 garlic cloves, crushed
1 tbsp dried mixed herbs
1 tbsp tomato purée
300ml/$\frac{1}{2}$pt red wine
1 tbsp cornflour
300ml/$\frac{1}{2}$pt cold water
2 small celeriac, peeled
25g/1oz butter

Preheat the oven to 200°C/400°F/Gas mark 6.

To make the sauce, mix together the yogurt, coriander, chilli and seasoning, then cover and chill until needed.

Cook the lamb in a large pan for a few minutes over a low heat until evenly browned, stirring occasionally. Add the onion and three-quarters of the garlic and cook for 2 minutes, stirring all the time. Add the seasoning, mixed herbs and tomato purée. Mix in the wine and simmer for 3 minutes.

Blend the cornflour with the water to form a paste, then stir into the lamb. Bring the mince to the boil so that it thickens, then transfer to a deep casserole dish.

Remove any blemishes from the celeriac and chop it into thin and even slices. Blanch the prepared celeriac in boiling water for

5 minutes. Drain and refresh under cold water.

Arrange a layer of celeriac over the mince, dot with butter, then add the remaining garlic and season. Cover with another layer of celeriac until it is all used up and dot with more butter. Bake until the celeriac is soft and cooked through and the top is golden brown. Reduce the heat to 180°C/350°F/Gas mark 4 and cook for a further 40 minutes. Serve hot with the sauce.

BEEF STEW

Serves 4

INGREDIENTS
450g/1lb shin of beef, cut into bite-sized cubes
1 tbsp olive oil
1 large onion, chopped
25g/1oz mushrooms, chopped
175g/6oz carrots, chopped
25g/1oz cornflour or rice flour
300ml/$1/2$pt beef stock
Salt and pepper
1 bay leaf

Preheat the oven to 140°C/275°F/Gas mark 1.

Brown the beef in a frying pan with the oil. Add the onion, mushroom and carrot and fry for a further 1 minute.

Mix the flour to a paste with a small amount of the stock and then continue to stir as you add the rest of the stock.

Place the beef and onion with the stock in a flameproof casserole dish. Add the herbs and seasoning. Bring to a simmer over a low heat.

Cover and cook slowly in the oven for 3 hours, checking at intervals to make sure it is gently simmering and adding more water if required.

FISH & SEAFOOD MAINS

If you are preparing a meal for guests then you are already worried enough about people enjoying your food, being told about a food intolerance just makes things even more complicated. However, if gluten-intolerance or coeliac disease is the problem, then this section may provide the solution. Among the various types of fish and seafood presented here are snapper, halibut, cod and prawns, to name but a few. And the methods of preparation are equally widely varied, from soufflés and bakes to curries and casseroles. So, whether it's an informal friendly meal or a sit-down dinner, these main courses are bound to go down swimmingly!

SALMON SOUFFLÉ

Serves 3

INGREDIENTS

1 tbsp butter, plus extra for greasing
2 tbsp gluten-free breadcrumbs
200g/7oz fresh salmon fillets
1 tbsp dry white vermouth
Salt and pepper
2 tbsp rice flour
3 tbsp single cream
3 egg yolks, beaten
5 egg whites

Preheat the oven to 200°C/400°F/Gas mark 6. Grease a large soufflé dish with butter, then coat with the breadcrumbs.

Poach the salmon in a little water with the vermouth and seasoning until just cooked through. Cool, remove the skin and any bones, then flake the fish, reserving the poaching liquid.

Melt the butter in a saucepan and beat in the flour. Add the poaching liquid and then the salmon and beat until smooth and thick. Bring to the boil and cook for 1 minute. Remove from the heat. Add the cream and egg yolks and mix well. Season with salt and pepper and pulse briefly in a blender or food processor until pale pink and smooth. Transfer to a bowl.

In a clean bowl, whisk the egg whites with a pinch of salt until firm. Stir one spoonful into the salmon and then quickly fold the rest in with a metal spoon. Spoon into the prepared dish.

Bake for 30 minutes until well risen and serve immediately.

GLAZED SNAPPER FILLETS

Serves 4

INGREDIENTS
2 tbsp lemon juice
2 tbsp olive oil
2 tbsp fruit chutney
1 tbsp clear honey
1 tbsp chopped fresh coriander
2 garlic cloves, crushed
4 snapper fillets

In a small bowl, combine the lemon juice, olive oil, fruit chutney, honey, coriander and garlic to make the marinade.

Place the snapper fillets in a non-metallic flat dish and pour the marinade over the top. Cover and refrigerate for 1¹/₂ hours.

Preheat the grill to high and put the fillets on the grill tray. Cook the fillets for about 5 minutes on each side, brushing occasionally with the remaining marinade. The snapper is ready for serving when it flakes easily with a fork.

BAKED TROUT

Serves 4

INGREDIENTS
Butter, for greasing
4 trout fillets, about 100g/4oz each, skinned
2 tbsp olive oil
50g/2oz pine nuts
1 small onion, chopped
200g/7oz baby spinach
1 garlic clove, sliced
25g/1oz Parmesan cheese, grated

Preheat the oven to 190°C/375°F/Gas mark 5.

Lightly butter a shallow ovenproof dish or roasting tin. Lay the
trout fillets in the dish, season lightly and drizzle with half of the
oil. Bake in the oven for 5 minutes.

Heat the remaining oil in a frying pan and fry the pine nuts and
onion for about 3 minutes until beginning to colour. Stir in the
spinach and garlic, and mix together until the spinach has
wilted.
Spoon the mixture over the trout and sprinkle with the cheese.
Return to the oven for a further 7 minutes until the fish is
cooked through.

FISH PIE

Serves 4

INGREDIENTS
900g/2lb potatoes, chopped
Salt and pepper
2 tbsp cornflour
$1/2$ tsp mustard
300ml/$1/2$pt milk
$1/2$ tsp grated lemon zest
$1/4$ tsp nutmeg
1 tsp lemon juice
1 tbsp chopped parsley
450g/1lb cod, cut into bite-sized pieces
50g/2oz fresh or frozen peas
100g/4oz prawns
50g/2oz canned sweetcorn, drained
Olive oil, for brushing

Preheat the oven to 200°C/400°F/Gas mark 6.

Boil the potatoes in water until soft. Drain, reserving the cooking water, then season and mash.

To make the white sauce, mix the cornflour and mustard with a little milk in a saucepan. Add the remaining milk, the lemon zest, nutmeg, lemon juice, parsley and 150ml/$1/4$pt of the potato cooking water. Bring to the boil, stirring constantly, then lower the heat and simmer for 2 minutes.

Add the cod to the sauce along with the peas, prawns and sweetcorn, and mix gently.

Place the fish mixture into a gratin dish and spread the mashed potato on top.

Brush the surface with olive oil and bake near the top of the oven for 30 minutes.

ROAST HALIBUT WITH BEETROOT PURÉE

Serves 2

INGREDIENTS
1 potato, cooked and mashed
2 tbsp milk
Salt and pepper
4 ready-cooked beetroots, chopped
1 garlic clove, crushed
1 tsp gluten-free vegetable stock powder
1/2 tsp ground cumin
1/2 tsp gluten-free mixed spice
250ml/9fl oz cold water
2 bay leaves
2 halibut steaks
Juice of 1/2 lemon

To make the beetroot purée, cook the potato in boiling water until soft, then mash with the milk and season. Place the beetroot, garlic, stock powder, cumin, mixed spice and water into a saucepan, bring to the boil, then lower the heat and simmer for 10 minutes.

Leave the mixture to cool slightly, then process it in a blender or food processor until it is smooth, but still thick. Mix the purée into the mashed potatoes and stir the mixture until it is an even texture and colour throughout.

Place the beetroot and potato mixture in a saucepan and heat through over a low heat.

Put the bay leaves on a baking tray and place the halibut on top. Season the fish and sprinkle on some of the lemon juice. Grill the fish for a few minutes under a high heat, then turn the halibut over and grill until just cooked through. Remove the bay leaves.

Place the hot purée in the centre of each plate and place the fish on top.

TUNA BALLS

Serves 4

INGREDIENTS
200g/7oz potatoes, mashed
300g/11oz canned tuna
3 eggs, separated
Salt and pepper
3 tbsp olive oil

Mix together the potatoes, tuna, egg yolks and seasoning.

Beat the egg whites for 5 minutes and add to the tuna mixture. Use your hands to make the mixture into ping-pong ball sized balls and fry in the oil until cooked through.

HADDOCK CASSEROLE

Serves 4

INGREDIENTS
1 carrot, grated
1/2 onion, grated
1 tbsp olive oil
4 haddock portions
150ml/1/4pt water
1 bay leaf
Salt and pepper
1 tbsp cornflour
150ml/1/4pt milk

Sweat the carrot and onion in the oil for 3 minutes. Add the haddock and turn to coat with the oil. Add the water, bay leaf and seasoning. Cover the pan and cook gently for about 10 minutes, until the fish is almost cooked.

Mix the cornflour and milk to a smooth paste and add to the pan, mixing with the juices and vegetables. Bring to the boil, cover and cook gently for another 5 minutes. Serve hot.

PRAWN CURRY

Serves 4

INGREDIENTS
675g/1¹/₂lb raw tiger prawns
1 tsp black mustard seeds
1 onion, chopped
4 dried red chillies
50g/2oz desiccated coconut
3 tbsp oil
4 bay leaves
2.5cm/1in piece fresh ginger, finely chopped
2 garlic cloves, crushed
1 tsp chilli powder
4 tomatoes, finely chopped
175ml/6fl oz water

Peel the prawns. Run a sharp knife along the back of each prawn to make a shallow cut and carefully remove the thin, black intestinal vein.

Put the mustard seeds, onion, chillies and coconut in a large frying pan and dry fry for 10 minutes or until the mixture begins to brown. Put into a blender or food processor and blend to a coarse paste.

Heat the oil in the frying pan and fry the bay leaves for 1 minute. Add the ginger and garlic and fry for 3 minutes. Add the chilli powder and coconut paste and fry for a further 5 minutes.

Stir in the tomatoes and water and simmer for 5 minutes, or until thickened.

Add the prawns and cook for 5 minutes, until they turn pink. Serve hot.

FISH KEBABS

Serves 4

INGREDIENTS
125ml/4fl oz olive oil
Grated zest and juice of 1 large lemon
1 tsp crushed chilli flakes
Salt and pepper
350g/12oz monkfish fillet, cubed
350g/12oz swordfish fillet, cubed
350g/12oz salmon fillet, cubed
2 red peppers, chopped
2 tbsp chopped fresh parsley

Put the oil in a shallow glass bowl and add the lemon zest and juice, chilli flakes and seasoning. Whisk to combine, then add the fish chunks. Turn to coat evenly. Add the red pepper, stir, then cover and leave to marinate in a cool place for 1 hour, turning occasionally.

Thread the fish and peppers on to eight skewers, reserving the marinade. Barbecue or grill the fish for 5 to 10 minutes, turning once.

Heat the reserved marinade, then remove from the heat and stir in the parsley, with seasoning to taste. Serve the kebabs hot with the marinade.

COD AND TOMATO BAKE

Serves 4

INGREDIENTS
Butter, for greasing
450g/1lb potatoes, cut into thin slices
2 tbsp olive oil
1 garlic clove, crushed
1 red onion, chopped
2 red peppers, diced
225g/8oz mushrooms, sliced
600g/1lb 5oz canned chopped tomatoes
150ml/^{1}/$_4$pt dry white wine
450g/1lb skinless, boneless cod fillet, cut into 2cm/^{3}/$_4$in cubes
50g/2oz pitted black olives, chopped
1 tbsp chopped fresh basil
1 tbsp chopped fresh oregano
Salt and pepper

Preheat the oven to 200°C/400°F/Gas mark 6. Lightly grease a large casserole dish with butter.

Par-boil the potatoes in a saucepan of lightly salted boiling water for 4 minutes. Drain thoroughly, then add 1 tablespoon oil and toss together to mix. Set aside.

Heat the remaining oil in a saucepan, add the garlic, onion and peppers and cook for 5 minutes, stirring occasionally.

Add the mushrooms, tomatoes and wine and bring to the boil. Boil rapidly for 3 minutes, or until the sauce has reduced slightly. Add the fish, olives, herbs and seasoning and mix together well. Spoon the mixture into the casserole dish and arrange the potato slices over the top.

Bake in the oven for about 45 minutes until the fish is cooked and tender and the potato topping is browned.

VEGGIE MAINS

Having a gluten-intolerance does not necessarily mean that you have to give up any other diet you have embarked upon by choice, including a vegetarian diet. Here is a great selection of meat-free dishes – including risottos, stews and salads – that are certainly brighter than your usual greens. So whether you have a vegetarian in the family, or just fancy getting some goodness into the children, you would do well to start here. Ingredients include sweet potatoes, tofu, lentils and even red wine! So whether you fancy a quiche, a roulade or ratatouille, look no further. It's all here, meat-free, gluten-free – and guilt-free!

NUT LOAF

Serves 4

INGREDIENTS
Butter, for greasing
2 garlic cloves, crushed
200g/7oz onion, chopped
25g/1oz vegetable oil
225g/8oz chopped hazelnuts
150g/5oz gluten-free breadcrumbs
2 eggs
Salt and pepper
150ml/¼pt water

Preheat the oven to 200°C/400°F/Gas mark 6. Grease a 450g/1lb
loaf tin with butter and line with greaseproof paper.

Fry the garlic and onion in the oil briefly until soft. Mix the
hazelnuts and breadcrumbs in a blender or food processor, then
combine with the onions and mix thoroughly in a large bowl.
Beat the eggs, seasoning and water into the mixture.

Place the mixture in the prepared loaf tin and bake in the oven
for 1 hour. Serve hot or cold.

Chinese-style pork (see page 36)

Above, Beef stir-fry (see page 41); Right, Fish kebabs (see page 60)

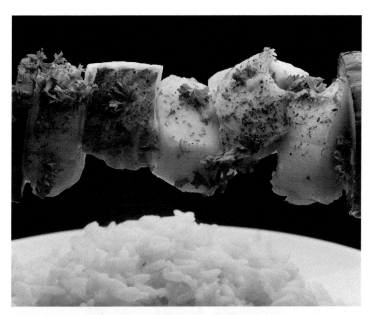

Above, Chicken kebabs (see page 46); Below, Glazed snapper fillets (see page 54)

67

Above, Chocolate cake (see page 111); Right, Lemon sponge roll (see page 112)

Above, Faity cakes (see page 114); Below, Chocolate mousse (see page 92)

Above, Lasagne (see page 45); Right, Pork with cherry sauce (see page 38)

Above, Chocolate chip cookies (see page 104); Below, Orange and tomato salad (see page 29)

Chicken casserole (see page 37)

MUSHROOM AND CHEESE RISOTTO

Serves 4

INGREDIENTS

10g/¼oz dried porcini mushrooms
150ml/¼pt hot water
1 tbsp olive oil
2 garlic cloves, crushed
4 shallots, finely chopped
450g/1lb button mushrooms
250g/9oz long-grain brown rice
900ml/1½pts vegetable stock
3 tbsp chopped fresh flat leaf parsley
50g/2oz Parmesan cheese, grated

Soak the porcini mushrooms in the hot water for 20 minutes.
Drain, reserving the soaking liquid, and chop roughly.

Heat the oil in a large saucepan, add the garlic and shallots and
cook gently for 5 minutes, stirring. Add the porcini and button
mushrooms to the pan along with the porcini soaking liquid, the
rice and 300ml/½pt stock.

Bring to the boil, then reduce the heat and simmer, uncovered,
until all the liquid has been absorbed, stirring frequently. Add a
ladleful of hot stock and stir until it has been absorbed.

Continue cooking and adding the hot stock, a ladleful at a time,
until the rice is cooked and creamy, stirring frequently. This
should take about 35 minutes. It may not be necessary to add all
the stock.

Stir in the parsley and sprinkle the Parmesan over the risotto
just before serving.

COURGETTE AND CAULIFLOWER BAKE

Serves 4

INGREDIENTS
Butter, for greasing
675g/1¹/₂lb cauliflower, divided into florets
3 tbsp rice flour
1 tsp mustard
150ml/¹/₄pt milk
3 eggs, separated
2 courgettes, cut into 1cm/¹/₂in slices
1 tbsp olive oil

Preheat the oven to 200°C/400°F/Gas mark 6. Grease a gratin tin with butter.

Cook the cauliflower for approximately 5 minutes in boiling water until just tender.

Mix the flour and mustard with the milk in a pan and bring to the boil, stirring constantly. Simmer for 1 minute.

Blend the cauliflower, egg yolks and white sauce in a blender or food processor until smooth.

Whisk the egg whites until stiff and fold into the cauliflower mixture with a large metal spoon.

Spoon half the mixture into the gratin tin. Arrange half the courgettes on top, then cover with the remaining cauliflower mixture. Top with the remaining courgettes and brush with the oil.

Bake in the oven for 30 minutes, or until golden brown.

CAULIFLOWER CHEESE

Serves 4

INGREDIENTS
1 cauliflower, cut into florets
25g/1oz cornflour
300ml/1/2pt milk
100g/4oz Cheddar cheese, grated
Salt and pepper

Place the cauliflower in a pan and cover with water and boil for 15 to 20 minutes, until tender. Drain the cauliflower and set aside.

Mix the cornflour into a paste with a little of the milk. Stir in the remaining milk without heating and add the cheese, then slowly heat the sauce to a simmer, stirring continuously, for 5 minutes.

Pour the sauce over the cauliflower and brown slightly under the grill before serving.

VEGETABLE AND BEAN STEW

Serves 6

INGREDIENTS
250g/9oz red kidney beans
900g/2lb butternut squash
3 courgettes, thickly sliced
3 red onions, chopped
1 medium aubergine, about 375g/13oz, cut into chunks
3 tbsp olive oil
1.2 litres/2pts vegetable stock
3 garlic cloves, sliced
2 bay leaves
2 tbsp chopped fresh oregano
2 tbsp ground paprika
300g/11oz button mushrooms

Preheat the oven to 220°C/425°F/Gas mark 7

Soak the kidney beans overnight in plenty of cold water. Drain, then cover with fresh water and bring to the boil. Boil rapidly for 10 minutes, then drain again.

Halve the squash, discard the seeds and cut away the skin. Cut the flesh into chunks and place in a large roasting tin with the courgettes, onions and aubergine. Drizzle with the oil and roast in the oven for 1 hour, turning the vegetables occasionally.

Place the beans in a large saucepan, add the stock, garlic, bay leaves, oregano and paprika, and bring to the boil. Reduce the heat, cover and simmer gently for 30 to 45 minutes until the beans are tender. Add the roasted vegetables to the pan with the mushrooms and cook for a further 5 minutes until heated through. Serve immediately.

TOFU RICE SALAD

Serves 4

INGREDIENTS
200g/7oz tofu, diced and cooked
200g/7oz brown rice, cooked
175g/6oz chopped pecans
100g/4oz golden raisins
150g/5oz onions, chopped
75ml/3fl oz olive oil
50ml/2fl oz rice vinegar
2 tbsp gluten-free soy sauce
1/4 tsp black pepper
4 lettuce leaves

Toss together all the ingredients except the lettuce leaves, then cover and chill for at least 1 hour.

Serve on a bed of lettuce leaves.

BEETROOT RISOTTO WITH RED WINE

Serves 6

INGREDIENTS
150g/5oz butter
2 large red onions, finely chopped
500g/1lb 2oz risotto rice
600ml/1pt red wine
Salt and pepper
1.2 litres/2pts hot vegetable stock
500g/1lb 2oz ready-cooked beetroots, cut into bite-sized pieces

In a large saucepan, melt 100g/4oz of the butter over a medium heat, add the onions and cook gently until nearly soft. Add the rice and stir for 1 minute. Pour in the wine, season to taste, and simmer for 5 minutes.

Pour the stock into the pan and simmer for 10 minutes. Stir the beetroot into the rice and simmer for a further 10 minutes and then fold in the remaining butter. Adjust the seasoning to taste and serve hot.

SWEET POTATO CASSEROLE

Serves 6

INGREDIENTS
25g/1oz butter, plus extra for greasing
1 large sweet potato
150g/5oz onion, chopped
150g/5oz red pepper, chopped
400g/14oz canned sweetcorn, drained
150g/5oz gluten-free cornflakes
200g/7oz Cheddar cheese, grated
50g/2oz Parmesan cheese, grated
Salt and pepper

Preheat the oven to 180°C/350°F/Gas mark 4. Lightly grease a
large casserole dish with butter.

Boil the sweet potato in water until soft and then mash.

Gently cook the onion, pepper and butter in a medium-
sized saucepan. Stir in the sweetcorn and sweet potato and half
the cornflakes. Blend together and place in the prepared
casserole dish.

Sprinkle the remaining cornflakes and cheeses over the top,
then bake, uncovered, for about 45 minutes until nicely browned
on top.

MUSHROOM AND PARMESAN RISOTTO

Serves 4

INGREDIENTS
15g/¹/₂oz dried porcini mushrooms
150ml/¹/₄pt hot water
1 tbsp olive oil
2 garlic cloves, crushed
4 shallots, finely chopped
450g/1lb closed cup mushrooms, sliced
250g/9oz long grain brown rice
900ml/1¹/₂pts vegetable stock
Salt and pepper
50g/2oz Parmesan cheese, grated

Soak the porcini mushrooms in the hot water for 20 minutes,
then drain, reserving the soaking liquid, and roughly chop.

Heat the oil in a large saucepan, add the garlic and shallots and
cook gently for 5 minutes, stirring. Add all the mushrooms to the
pan along with the porcini soaking liquid, the brown rice and
300ml/¹/₂pt stock.

Bring to the boil, reduce the heat and simmer, uncovered, until
all the liquid has been absorbed, stirring frequently. Add a
ladleful of hot stock and stir until it has been absorbed. Continue
cooking and adding the hot stock, a little at a time, stirring
frequently for 30 minutes until the rice is cooked. It may not be
necessary to add all the stock.

Season with salt and pepper to taste, stir in the Parmesan and
serve at once.

VEGGIE MAINS

LENTIL BOLOGNESE

Serves 4

INGREDIENTS

100g/4oz brown lentils
1/2 green pepper, finely chopped
1 carrot, diced
1 tsp dried oregano
1 tsp dried basil
1 celery stick, chopped
1 onion, finely chopped
2 garlic cloves, crushed
600ml/1pt tomato juice
300ml/1/2pt water
1 bay leaf
Salt and pepper

Place the lentils in a saucepan with the pepper, carrot, oregano, basil, celery, onion, garlic and bay leaf. Add the tomato juice and water, bring to the boil and simmer, covered, for 30 minutes or until the lentils are soft. Remove the bay leaf, stir well and season to taste. Serve hot.

VEGETABLE MOUSSAKA

Serves 6

INGREDIENTS
450g/1lb aubergines, sliced
Salt and pepper
150g/5oz whole green lentils
600ml/1pt vegetable stock
1 bay leaf
3 tbsp olive oil
1 garlic clove, crushed
1 onion, sliced
250g/9oz mushrooms, sliced
400g/14oz canned chickpeas, drained
400g/14oz canned chopped tomatoes
2 tbsp tomato purée
2 tsp dried mixed herbs
3 tbsp water
3 eggs
250ml/9fl oz natural yogurt
75g/3oz Cheddar cheese, grated

Sprinkle the aubergine with salt and place in a colander. Cover and leave for 30 minutes to drain.

Place the lentils, stock and bay leaf in a saucepan. Cover, bring to the boil and simmer for about 20 minutes until the lentils are just tender. Drain well and keep warm.

Heat 1 tbsp oil in a large saucepan, add the garlic and onion and cook for 5 minutes, stirring. Stir in the lentils, mushrooms, chickpeas, tomatoes, tomato purée, herbs and water. Bring to the boil, cover and simmer gently for 10 minutes.

Meanwhile, preheat the oven to 180°C/350°F/Gas mark 4.

Rinse the aubergine and pat dry. Heat the remaining oil in a frying pan and fry the slices in batches for 4 minutes, turning once.

Arrange a layer of aubergine slices in the bottom of a large, shallow roasting tin, then spoon over a layer of the lentil mixture. Continue the layers until all the aubergine slices and lentil mixture are used up.

Beat together the eggs, yogurt and seasoning and pour the mixture into the dish. Sprinkle the cheese on top and bake for about 45 minutes until the topping is golden brown. Serve immediately.

TOFU CUTLETS

Serves 4

INGREDIENTS
450g/1lb firm tofu
50ml/2fl oz lime juice
3 tbsp gluten-free soy sauce
1 tbsp sesame oil
1 tbsp clear honey
1 tbsp chopped onion
1 tbsp crushed garlic
1 tsp black pepper
2 tbsp sesame seeds

Slice the tofu into four pieces lengthwise.

Combine all the other ingredients except the sesame seeds to create a marinade. Add the tofu to the marinade and refrigerate for 2 to 4 hours, turning occasionally. Remove from the refrigerator and allow to return to room temperature.

Preheat the oven to 180°C/350°F/Gas mark 4 and sprinkle the tofu with the sesame seeds. Bake in the oven for 45 minutes and serve hot.

BROCCOLI QUICHE

Serves 4

INGREDIENTS
8 large cabbage leaves
400g/14oz broccoli florets
2 onions, chopped
1 tbsp olive oil
1 tbsp chopped fresh parsley
3 eggs
450ml/³/4pt milk
Salt and pepper
225g/8oz sweetcorn kernels
50g/2oz ground hazelnuts

Preheat the oven to 200°C/400°F/Gas mark 6.

Cook the cabbage and the broccoli in boiling water for about 5 minutes until the cabbage leaves are soft enough to line the dish and the broccoli is still crunchy.

Cool the broccoli quickly by dipping in cold water to prevent overcooking. Sweat the onions in the oil until they begin to brown and soften. Mix in the parsley.

Beat the eggs and milk and season with salt and pepper.

Use the cabbage leaves to double-line a deep 25cm/10in quiche dish. Scatter half the onions over the base, then arrange the broccoli florets around the dish.

Fill the gaps between the broccoli with sweetcorn, then scatter the remaining onions on top. Pour over the egg and milk mixture and scatter the ground nuts over the surface.

Bake in the oven for approximately 45 minutes or until the centre of the quiche is just setting. Do not over cook or the eggs will start to curdle and spoil the quiche.

LEEK AND ORANGE LOAF

Serves 4

INGREDIENTS
Butter, for greasing
4 oranges, sliced
675g/1¹/₂lb prepared leeks, chopped
100g/4oz butter
6 medium eggs, separated
Salt and pepper
2 tbsp finely chopped parsley
50g/2oz Cheddar cheese, grated

Preheat the oven to 180°C/350°F/Gas mark 4. Lightly grease a
shallow baking tin.

Simmer the oranges gently in their own juice, adding a little
water if necessary. Liquidize the cooked oranges in a blender or
food processor.

Cook the leeks in the butter until soft and golden. Mix the leeks
with the oranges.

Beat in the egg yolks, one at a time into the leek and orange. Add
the seasoning and parsley.

Beat the egg whites with a pinch of salt until stiff, then fold into
the mixture. Gently spread the mixture in the prepared baking tin.

Bake in the oven for 25 minutes. Sprinkle with the cheese to serve.

NUT ROULADE

Serves 6

INGREDIENTS

75g/3oz butter, plus extra for greasing
350g/12oz parsnips, chopped
2 tbsp single cream
Salt and pepper
400g/14oz canned sweetcorn, drained
25g/1oz rice flour
300ml/½pt milk
1 tsp fresh thyme leaves
150g/5oz courgettes, grated
75g/3oz chopped mixed nuts
2 eggs, separated

Preheat the oven to 200°C/400°F/Gas mark 6. Grease a large non-stick roulade tin with butter, then line with greaseproof paper.

Boil the parsnips until soft. Drain and then mash them with 25g/1oz butter and the cream until smooth. Season to taste with salt and pepper. Stir in the sweetcorn, cover and keep warm.

To make the roulade, melt the remaining butter, then beat in the flour and then incorporate the milk until you have a smooth sauce. Season to taste with thyme, salt and pepper. Stir in the courgette, half the mixed nuts and the egg yolks and remove from the heat.

In a large bowl, whisk the egg whites until stiff, then fold into the mixture carefully using a metal spoon. Scrape the mixture into the prepared tin and bake for 20 minutes. Turn the roulade on to a piece of greaseproof paper that has been sprinkled with the remaining nuts.

Peel off the greaseproof paper. Spread the warm filling mixture over the roulade and use the paper to help roll the roulade.

LENTIL CASSEROLE

Serves 6

INGREDIENTS
1 tbsp sunflower oil
1 garlic clove, crushed
2 leeks, sliced
4 celery sticks, chopped
1 sweet potato, diced
2 carrots, sliced
2 parsnips, diced
225g/8oz swede, diced
175g/6oz brown lentils
400g/14oz canned chopped tomatoes
2 tbsp chopped fresh thyme
900ml/1½pts vegetable stock
1 tbsp cornflour
3 tbsp water
Salt and pepper

Preheat the oven to 180°C/350°F/Gas mark 4.

Heat the oil in a large flameproof casserole dish. Add the garlic, leeks and celery and cook over a low heat for 3 minutes, stirring occasionally.

Add the sweet potato, carrots, parsnips, swede, lentils, tomatoes, thyme, stock and seasoning. Stir well. Bring to the boil, stirring occasionally.

Cover and bake for 50 minutes, or until the vegetables and lentils are tender stirring a couple of times during cooking.

Remove the casserole from the oven. Blend the cornflour with the water in a small bowl. Stir it into the casserole and heat gently, stirring continuously, until the mixture comes to the boil, then simmer gently for 2 minutes, stirring. Season to taste and serve hot.

RATATOUILLE

Serves 6

INGREDIENTS

450g/1lb aubergines, cut into 2.5cm/1in slices
75ml/3fl oz olive oil
1 large onion, halved and sliced
1 red pepper, cut into thin strips
3 garlic cloves, crushed
2 courgettes, cut into 1cm/$\frac{1}{2}$in slices
400g/14oz canned chopped tomatoes
1 tsp dried mixed herbs
Salt and pepper

Brush the aubergine slices with oil on both sides. Grill until lightly browned, turning once, then cut into chunks.

Heat 1 tablespoon oil in a large casserole dish and cook the onion for about 10 minutes, stirring frequently. Add the pepper, garlic and courgettes and cook for a further 10 minutes.

Add the tomatoes, aubergine, dried herbs and seasoning. Simmer gently, covered, over a low heat for about 20 minutes, stirring occasionally. Uncover and continue cooking for a further 25 minutes, stirring occasionally, until all the vegetables are tender. Serve hot.

DESSERTS

You most certainly do not have to give up these sweet things if you suffer from coeliac disease. Nothing rounds off a meal quite as well as a delicious dessert and, for those with a sweet tooth, sometimes a pudding can be a sneaky indulgence, a treat to be eaten without having to eat a meal first! And a wonderfully wide selection of treats can be found here, from the mouth-watering to the delicious and decadent. Chocolate-lovers will find mousse and cookies to fulfil their passion, while gingerbread, macaroons and trifle will tempt even the strictest dieter.

GINGERBREAD

Serves 10

INGREDIENTS

125ml/4fl oz black treacle
50g/2oz butter
1 tsp bicarbonate of soda
50g/2oz dark brown sugar
$^1/_2$ tsp ground cloves
$^1/_2$ tsp ground cinnamon
1 tsp ground ginger
1 large egg
150g/5oz rice flour
150g/5oz potato flour, plus extra for dusting

Preheat the oven to 180°C/350°F/Gas mark 4.

In a saucepan, over a medium heat, combine the treacle and butter, then melt them together. Remove from the heat, allow the mixture to cool down, then transfer to a large bowl and add the bicarbonate of soda, sugar, cloves, cinnamon, ginger, egg and flours. Beat with a wooden spoon for 2 minutes.

Transfer the dough on to a floured board and knead with a little extra flour until you can roll it with a floured rolling pin. Roll the dough until it is thin enough to cut into shapes.

Place the gingerbread shapes on non-stick baking trays at least 1cm/$^1/_2$in apart. Bake for 12 minutes, or until firm. Transfer to wire racks to cool completely.

PEAR BROWNIE

Serves 6

INGREDIENTS

75g/3oz butter, plus extra for greasing
800g/1lb 12oz canned pears in juice
75g/3oz rice flour
Pinch of salt
1 tsp baking powder
1/2 tsp vanilla essence
100g/4oz dark chocolate, broken into squares
175g/6oz caster sugar
2 large eggs, beaten
75g/3oz chopped pecan nuts

Preheat the oven to 180°C/350°F/Gas mark 4. Grease a deep
baking dish with butter.

Cover the base of the baking dish with the pears.

Sift the flour, salt and baking powder into a bowl. Put the butter,
vanilla essence and chocolate into a saucepan, stir until melted
and then remove from the heat.

Beat in the sugar, eggs and nuts, then fold in the flour. Add to the
baking dish and bake in the oven for about 30 minutes or until
firm. The brownies are best served warm.

CHOCOLATE MOUSSE

Serves 6

INGREDIENTS

225g/8oz plain chocolate, broken into squares
2 tbsp brandy
4 eggs, separated
6 tbsp double cream

Line a shallow 20cm/8in round cake tin with clingfilm. Melt the chocolate in a bowl over a pan of simmering water, then remove from the heat.

Beat the brandy and egg yolks into the chocolate, then fold in the cream, mixing well. In a clean bowl, whisk the egg whites until stiff, then gently fold them into the chocolate mixture.

Pour the mixture into the prepared tin and level the surface. Chill for several hours until set.

LEMON CREAM

Serves 4

INGREDIENTS
15g/½oz powdered gelatine
150ml/¼pt hot water
175g/6oz granulated sugar
Juice of 2 lemons
2 eggs, separated
300ml/½pt milk

Sprinkle the gelatine over the water and stir until it has dissolved. Add the sugar and stir until dissolved. Allow to cool until just warm. Add the lemon juice.

Beat the egg yolks and then stir into the gelatine solution. Stir the milk into the mixture, keeping it warm over a gentle heat. Remove the mixture from the heat.

In a clean bowl whisk the egg whites and fold into the mixture. Pour into a bowl and place in the refrigerator until set.

ARROWROOT BISCUITS

Serves 12

INGREDIENTS

75g/3oz butter, plus extra for greasing
100g/4oz granulated sugar
1 egg
1/2 tsp vanilla essence
200g/7oz white rice flour, plus extra for dusting
75g/3oz tapioca flour
50g/2oz potato starch flour
100g/4oz arrowroot flour
1/2 tsp gluten-free baking powder
1/4 tsp salt

Preheat the oven to 180°C/350°F/Gas mark 4. Lightly grease a baking tray with butter.

Cream together the butter and sugar, then beat in the egg and vanilla. Add the remaining ingredients and mix to form a dough.

Knead the dough until smooth, then roll out on to a floured surface. Cut the biscuits with a 5cm/2in cutter and place on the prepared baking tray. Prick with fork and bake in the oven for 8 to 10 minutes

MACAROONS

Serves 10

INGREDIENTS

2 egg whites
100g/4oz caster sugar
100g/4oz ground almonds
10 blanched almonds

Preheat the oven to 180°C/350°F/Gas mark 4. Line a large baking tray with greaseproof paper.

Whisk the egg whites until stiff, then gradually whisk in the sugar, a little at a time, until the mixture is thick and glossy. Stir in the ground almonds.

Spoon the mixture into a piping bag. Pipe small rounds on to the baking tray about 5cm/2in in diameter, spacing them slightly apart. Press a blanched almond into the top of each one.

Bake in the oven for 15 to 20 minutes until only just firm. Leave on the paper to cool.

AMARETTI

Serves 10

INGREDIENTS
400g/14oz blanched slivered almonds
300g/11oz granulated sugar
3 egg whites
1 tsp almond extract

Preheat the oven to 180°C/350°F/Gas mark 4. Line baking trays with greaseproof paper.

In a blender or food processor, grind the almonds into a fine meal. Add the sugar and continue to process for another 15 seconds. Finally, add the egg whites and almond extract, continue to process until a smooth dough forms around the blade.

Using a teaspoon, place well-rounded spoonfuls of dough on to the prepared baking sheets. Bake in the oven for 20 to 30 minutes, or until golden.

APPLE TART

Serves 10

INGREDIENTS

150g/5oz butter, plus extra for greasing
150g/5oz rice flour, plus extra for dusting
150g/5oz maize flour
50g/2oz caster sugar
Pinch of salt
1 large egg
2 tbsp cold water
500ml/16fl oz apple purée
3 large sweet dessert apples, peeled, cored and quartered
100g/4oz apricot jam

Preheat the oven to 200°C/400°F/Gas mark 6. Grease a 30cm/12in loose-bottomed tart tin with butter and dust with rice flour.

Combine the flours, butter, sugar, salt and egg together in a blender or food processor with the water. Process until it forms a dough.

Put the pastry into the middle of the prepared tin and gently flatten it until it reaches the sides. Trim the pastry with a knife and discard the trimmings.

Pour the apple purée into the pastry shell and smooth over. Slice the apple quarters horizontally into wafer thin slices and arrange in overlapping circles.

Bake the tart for 45 minutes, or until the apples are browned and tender. Keep in the tin while it cools down.

Heat the jam over a low heat and spread over the apples. Once the tart is cold, remove it carefully from the tin and serve.

CRÊPES SUZETTES

Serves 8

INGREDIENTS
50g/2oz rice flour
50g/2oz barley flour
Pinch of salt
3 large eggs
300ml/1/2pt milk
150g/5oz butter, plus extra for frying
Sunflower oil for frying
4 tbsp icing sugar
1 tbsp grated orange zest
2 tbsp fresh orange juice, strained
1 tbsp orange liqueur
Caster sugar, for dusting
3 tbsp brandy

To make the crêpes, sift the flours into a bowl with the salt, then make a well in the centre. Break the eggs into the well and whisk until thoroughly mixed.

Melt 25g/1oz butter and combine with the milk, then add to the bowl in a steady stream, whisking to make a smooth paste. Leave the batter to stand for 30 minutes.

Heat a little oil in an 18cm/7in crêpe pan. Ladle a tablespoon of the crêpe mixture into the pan and swirl it around so that the base of the pan is evenly coated. Cook until crispy and golden, flipping once, so both sides are cooked. Continue until all the batter is gone.

Make the filling by mixing the remaining butter and icing sugar together in a blender or food processor until pale and light. Add the orange zest and juice with the liqueur and blend until smooth. Spread the filling over each crêpe and fold into a triangle. Heat a little butter in a large frying pan, add the crêpes and dust with caster sugar. Pour the brandy over and set light to it. Cook until the flames go out and then serve immediately.

RASPBERRY AND PEACH CRUMBLE

Serves 4

INGREDIENTS

50g/2oz butter, plus extra for greasing
75g/3oz rice flour
25g/1oz buckwheat flakes
25g/1oz millet flakes
25g/1oz hazelnuts, roughly chopped
75g/3oz soft light brown sugar
1 tsp ground ginger
225g/8oz raspberries
3 fresh peaches, cut into wedges
4 tbsp fresh orange juice

Preheat the oven to 180°C/350°F/Gas mark 4. Grease a
1.2 litre/2pt pie dish with butter.

To make the crumble, place the flour in bowl and rub in the
butter until the mixture resembles breadcrumbs.

Stir in the buckwheat flakes, millet flakes, hazelnuts, 50g/2oz
sugar and the ginger. Mix together thoroughly.

Mix the raspberries, peaches, orange juice and remaining sugar
together and place in the dish. Sprinkle the crumble over the top,
pressing it down lightly. Bake for 30 to 45 minutes. Can be served
warm or cold.

COFFEE TRIFLE

Serves 6

INGREDIENTS
125ml/4fl oz strong black coffee, cooled
50ml/2fl oz coffee-flavoured liqueur
200g/7oz cream cheese
500ml/18fl oz custard
200g/7oz gluten-free macaroons [see page 94]
50g/2oz milk chocolate, coarsely grated
25g/1oz flaked almonds, lightly toasted

Mix the coffee with the liqueur in a jug.

Beat the cream cheese and custard together in a bowl until the mixture is completely smooth.

Arrange half the macaroons in the base of a 1.2 litre/2pt glass serving dish and drizzle with half the coffee mixture. Put the remaining macaroons in a single layer on a plate and drizzle the remaining syrup over them.

Scatter half the chocolate and half the almonds over the biscuits in the bowl. Spoon over half the cheese mixture.

Layer the syrup-covered macaroons, chocolate and almonds in the dish. Pile the remaining cheese mixture on top and chill until ready to serve.

MANGO MOUSSE

Serves 12

INGREDIENTS
Seeds from 10 cardamom pods
6 large egg yolks
2 tbsp caster sugar
450ml/3/4pt double cream
3 tbsp orange liqueur
2 mangos, peeled, stoned and roughly chopped
Juice of 1 orange
Juice of 1 lemon
25g/1oz powdered gelatine
50ml/2fl oz boiling water
3 egg whites
5 ripe passion fruit, halved, seeds and juices scooped out and
used for decoration

Put the cardamom seeds into a non-stick saucepan with the egg
yolks and sugar and beat with a wooden spoon. Gradually add
the cream. Cool the mixture over a low heat until it thickens and
comes almost to boiling point, stirring constantly. Remove from
the heat and continue to stir.

Add the liqueur and leave the custard to cool in a clean bowl,
stirring occasionally.

Purée the mango and fruit juices together in a blender or food
processor until smooth, then stir the purée into the custard.
Dissolve the gelatine in the boiling water, then stir into the
mixture, and set aside until the mixture is cold.

Whisk the egg whites in a separate bowl until they form stiff
peaks. Fold the egg white mixture into the custard using a metal
spoon and transfer to a freezerproof dish. Freeze for 40 minutes.

Remove the mouse from the freezer and cover with clingfilm.
Chill in the refrigerator for 4 hours, until it is firm and set.

Decorate the mousse with passion fruit. Serve chilled.

PEPPERMINT CREAMS

Serves 10

INGREDIENTS

450g/1lb icing sugar, plus extra for dusting
2 tsp water
1 tsp lemon juice
1 large egg white, lightly whisked
1 tsp peppermint flavouring or oil

Mix the sugar with the water, lemon juice and enough egg white to make a pliable mixture. Flavour the mixture with the peppermint.

Knead on a clean surface, dusted with icing sugar, and then gently roll out the mixture into a long sausage shape.

Slice the dough into neat rounds or form into balls and flatten slightly with the back of a fork.

Leave somewhere cool for 24 hours, until thoroughly dry.

RICE PUDDING

Serves 4

INGREDIENTS
75g/3oz dessert rice
600ml/1pt water
600ml/1pt milk
50g/2oz granulated sugar
2 eggs
1 drop vanilla essence
25g/1oz nutmeg, grated

Preheat the oven to 180°C/350°F/Gas mark 4

Boil the rice in the water for 5 minutes. Leave to stand for 10 minutes, then drain.

Beat together the milk, sugar and eggs with the vanilla essence. Add the rice to the mixture.

Place the mixture in an ovenproof bowl and sprinkle nutmeg on top. Stand the bowl in a deep baking tray of water in the oven. The water should come halfway up the bowl.

Bake in the oven for 1¹/₂ hours, or until just set.

BLACKCURRANT SORBET

Serves 6

INGREDIENTS
300ml/¹/₂pt water
100g/4oz caster sugar
225g/8oz fresh or frozen blackcurrants
1 tsp lemon juice
2 tbsp blackcurrant liqueur

Pour the water into a saucepan and add the sugar. Place over a low heat and stir until the sugar has dissolved. Bring to the boil and boil rapidly for 10 minutes, then set aside to cool.

Cook the blackcurrants in a saucepan with 2 tablespoons water over a low heat for 6 minutes until tender. Press the blackcurrants and their juice through a sieve placed over a jug and stir into the sugar syrup with the lemon juice and the blackcurrant liqueur. Allow to cool completely, then chill in the refrigerator for 1 hour.

Pour into a freezerproof bowl and freeze for 3 hours, or until slushy, whisking occasionally, then spoon into a blender or food processor and process. Alternately freeze and process until completely smooth. Serve straight from the freezer.

BAKED APPLES AND BANANAS

Serves 4

INGREDIENTS
2 dessert apples, peeled, cored and thinly sliced
2 bananas, split lengthwise and halved
Juice of 1/2 lemon
100g/4oz dark brown sugar
100g/4oz light brown sugar
250ml/9fl oz apple juice
1/2 tsp ground cinnamon
1 tsp vanilla essence

Preheat the oven to 200°C/400°F/Gas mark 6.

Combine the apples and bananas and place in a shallow baking dish, then sprinkle with lemon juice.

Combine the remaining ingredients except the vanilla essence in a saucepan and boil until the sugar is dissolved. Remove from the heat, add the vanilla, and pour over the bananas and apples. Bake in the oven for 20 minutes, or until bubbling.

CHOCOLATE CHIP COOKIES

Serves 8

INGREDIENTS

75g/3oz butter, plus extra for greasing
50g/2oz light soft brown sugar
50g/2oz caster sugar
1 egg, beaten
1/4 tsp vanilla essence
75g/3oz rice flour
1 tsp gluten-free baking powder
75g/3oz gluten-free cornmeal
100g/4oz plain chocolate chips

Preheat the oven to 190°C/375°F/Gas mark 5. Lightly grease two baking trays with butter.

Place the butter and sugars in a bowl and cream together.

Beat in the egg and vanilla essence. Fold in the flour, baking powder and cornmeal, then fold in the chocolate chips.

Place spoonfuls of the mixture on the prepared baking trays, leaving space for spreading between each one. Bake for 10 to 15 minutes.

Remove from the oven and leave to cool for a few minutes, then transfer to a wire rack and leave to cool completely before serving.

GINGERSNAPS

Serves 10

INGREDIENTS
75g/3oz butter, plus extra for greasing
100g/4oz sugar
75g/3oz soya flour
75g/3oz cornflour
75g/3oz potato starch flour
1/4 tsp salt
1 tbsp gluten-free baking powder
1/4 tsp grated fresh ginger
1/2 tsp fresh cinnamon
2 tbsp molasses
1 egg

Preheat the oven to 180°C/350°F/Gas mark 4. Grease two baking trays with butter.

Sift the sugar, flours, salt and baking powder together, then mix in the ginger and cinnamon.

Cream together the butter and sugar thoroughly. Beat in the egg and molasses, then add the flour mixture and mix well.

Drop rounded teaspoons of dough on to the prepared baking trays. Bake in the oven for 10 to 12 minutes.

CAKES

When diagnosed with a gluten intolerance or coeliac disease, one of the first foods you were warned to stay away from was probably cakes. With gluten occurring in several grains and flours, it is often difficult to guarantee that any cake is gluten-free. Unless, of course, you make one yourself, following the recipes in this section. Whether you fancy a classic Victoria sandwich, or something a little different – like a walnut syrup cake, or a banana sponge – this is the place to find it. There is also a recipe for Christmas cake, so your holiday season can include as much tasty fun as everyone else's.

VICTORIA SANDWICH CAKE

Serves 10

INGREDIENTS
175g/6oz butter, plus extra for greasing
175g/6oz caster sugar
3 eggs, beaten
175g/6oz gluten-free self-raising flour, sifted
4 tbsp strawberry jam
150ml/¼pt whipped cream
2 tbsp icing sugar, sifted

Preheat the oven to 180°C/350°F/Gas mark 4. Lightly grease two 18cm/7in sandwich tins with butter and line with greaseproof paper.

Place the butter and caster sugar in a bowl and cream together.

Add the eggs, a little at a time, beating well after each addition. Fold in the flour, using a metal spoon.

Divide the mixture evenly between the prepared tins and level the surface.

Bake for 25 to 30 minutes until the cakes have risen and are golden brown. Cool on a wire rack.

When the cakes are cool, sandwich them with the jam and whipped cream. Dust the top of the cake with the icing sugar and serve cut into slices.

SOUR CREAM CAKE

Serves 10

INGREDIENTS

For the cake:
75g/3oz butter, plus extra for greasing
300g/11oz rice flour, plus extra for dusting
200g/7oz sugar
2 eggs
2 tsp gluten-free baking powder
250ml/9fl oz sour cream
1 tsp vanilla essence

For the topping:
150g/5oz light brown sugar
1 tbsp cinnamon
2 tbsp rice flour
2 tbsp butter, melted
50g/2oz chopped nuts

Preheat the oven to 180°C/350°F/Gas mark 4. Grease a 30cm/12in cake pan with butter and dust with flour.

Cream together the butter and sugar. Add the eggs one at a time, beating well after each. Add the flour, and baking powder alternately with the sour cream and vanilla essence.

In a separate bowl, combine the topping ingredients together.

Pour half the batter into the prepared cake pan, add half the topping, then repeat. Bake in the oven for 35 to 40 minutes.

CHOCOLATE CAKE

Serves 10

INGREDIENTS
100g/4oz butter, plus extra for greasing
100g/4oz plain chocolate, broken into small pieces
100g/4oz caster sugar
4 eggs, separated
75g/3oz ground almonds
25g/1oz potato flour

Preheat the oven to 160°C/325°F/Gas mark 3. Grease a 20cm/8in cake tin with butter and line with greaseproof paper.

Melt the chocolate in a mixing bowl over a pan of simmering water. Remove from the heat and whisk in the butter and sugar, egg yolks and almonds.

In a separate bowl whisk the egg whites until they form stiff peaks and then fold into the mixture together with the flour.

Put the mixture into the prepared cake tin and bake in the oven for about 1 hour.

Let the cake cool in the tin before turning out.

LEMON SPONGE ROLL

Serves 12

INGREDIENTS

Butter, for greasing
Grated zest and juice of 1 lemon
100g/4oz granulated sugar
3 eggs, separated
100g/4oz rice flour
75g/3oz cornflour
1½ tsp gluten-free baking powder
3 tbsp caster sugar (added to whites)
¼ tsp cream of tartar

For the filling:
100g/4oz caster sugar
3 egg yolks
Grated zest and juice of 2 lemons
50g/2oz butter
400ml/14fl oz whipped cream, whipped

Preheat the oven to 180°C/350°F/Gas mark 4. Grease a Swiss roll tin with butter and line with greaseproof paper.

Combine the lemon zest with the granulated sugar. In a mixing bowl, beat the egg yolks with the sugar and zest mixture until the yolks have increased in volume. Add the lemon juice and beat to combine.

Combine the flour, cornflour and baking powder, and blend with the yolk mixture.

In a large bowl, beat the egg whites and 1 tablespoon caster sugar until they are frothy. Add the cream of tartar and continue beating until whites are stiff. Fold into the flour mixture.

Spread the mixture into the prepared tin and bake for 15 to 20 minutes or until the cake is light brown. Turn the cake on to a tea towel and roll up, using the tea towel as a guide. Peel off the greaseproof paper and place the cake seam-side down on to a wire rack and allow to cool completely.

To make the filling, combine the sugar and the yolks in a small saucepan. Add the lemon juice, slowly, and cook over a medium heat, stirring constantly until it thickens. Remove from the heat and whisk in the butter and zest. Bring to room temperature and fold in the whipped cream.

Unroll the cake and spread with an even layer of filling. Roll the cake back up and sprinkle with the remaining caster sugar before serving.

ANGEL CAKE

Serves 10

INGREDIENTS
Butter, for greasing
150g/5oz rice flour, sifted
175g/6oz caster sugar
Pinch of salt
7 egg whites
2 tsp cream of tartar
1 tbsp rosewater
100g/4oz raspberries
150g/5oz strawberries, quartered
100g/4oz blackberries
2 tbsp white rum
2 tbsp granulated sugar

Preheat the oven to 180°C/350°F/Gas mark 4. Grease a 20cm/8in cake tin with butter.

Sift together the flour, half the caster sugar and the salt in a bowl and set aside. In another large bowl, whisk the egg whites until they are thick. Add the cream of tartar and whisk for a further 1 minute.

Slowly sprinkle 2 tablespoons caster sugar into the egg whites and beat them until they form soft peaks. Add the rosewater and fold in the remaining caster sugar, followed by the flour mixture.

Pour the mixture into the tin and bake in the oven for about 40 minutes, or until golden and firm to touch.

Leave to cool in the tin for 20 minutes, then turn it out on to a serving plate.

Fill the centre of the cake with half the raspberries, strawberries and blackberries. Place the remaining berries in a blender or food processor with the rum and granulated sugar and purée to make a sauce. Sieve the sauce and discard all the pips and skins.

Serve with the sauce spooned generously over the cake.

FAIRY CAKES

Serves 9

INGREDIENTS
50g/2oz ground almonds
75g/3oz gluten-free plain flour
1 tsp gluten-free baking powder
100g/4oz golden caster sugar
100g/4oz unsalted butter, softened
2 eggs

Preheat the oven to 180°C/350°F/Gas mark 4. Line tartlet trays with 18 paper cases.

Put the almonds, flour, baking powder, sugar, butter and eggs in a large bowl. Beat with a hand-held electric whisk for about 2 minutes until smooth and creamy.

Using teaspoons, divide the mixture among the paper cases. Bake in the oven for 20 to 30 minutes until golden and just firm to touch. Transfer to a wire rack to cool.

CHOCOLATE PRUNE CAKE

Serves 10

INGREDIENTS
150g/5oz butter, plus extra for greasing
300g/11oz dark chocolate
200g/7oz ready-to-eat stoned prunes, quartered
3 eggs, beaten
150g/5oz gram flour
2 tsp gluten-free baking powder
125ml/4fl oz milk

Preheat the oven to 180°C/350°F/Gas mark 4. Grease a deep
20cm/8in round cake tin with butter and line with greaseproof
paper.

Melt the chocolate in a bowl over a saucepan of simmering
water. Mix the butter and prunes in a blender or food processor.
Process until fluffy, then scrape into a bowl.

Sift the flour and baking powder together and fold in the melted
chocolate and eggs, alternately with the flour mixture, into the
prunes. Beat in the milk.

Spoon the mixture into the prepared cake tin, level the surface,
then bake in the oven for about 30 minutes or until the cake is
firm. A skewer inserted should come out clean. Leave to cool on a
wire rack before serving.

MINI SOUR CREAM CHEESECAKES

Serves 8

INGREDIENTS
700g/1½lb cream cheese
200g/7oz granulated sugar
5 eggs
1 tsp vanilla essence

For the topping:
225g/8oz sour cream
200g/7oz granulated sugar
1 tsp vanilla essence

Preheat the oven to 180°C/350°F/Gas mark 4. Line 8 muffin tins with greaseproof paper.

In a medium-sized bowl, cream together the cream cheese and sugar. Stir in the eggs one at a time, then mix in the vanilla essence. Spoon into cupcake pans to fill about three-quarters full.

Bake for 30 minutes in the oven, until golden brown. Remove from the oven and cool for 5 to 10 minutes.

To make topping, whisk together the sour cream, sugar and vanilla essence until smooth. Spoon into the well on the top of each cupcake.

Return to the oven and bake for an additional 5 minutes, until set. Place on a wire rack to cool completely before serving.

BLUEBERRY MUFFINS

Serves 6

INGREDIENTS

Butter, for greasing
250g/9oz rice flour
2 tsp gluten-free baking powder
1 tsp bicarbonate of soda
175g/6oz instant gluten-free polenta
2 tbsp granulated sugar
250g/9oz dried blueberries
175g/6oz soya yogurt with live ferments
2 tbsp lemon juice
Grated zest of 1 lemon
1 tbsp corn oil
225g/8oz canned crushed pineapple in natural juice, drained
25ml/1fl oz apple juice

Preheat the oven to 200°C/400°F/Gas mark 6. Grease a 12-hole
muffin tray with butter.

Sift the flour, baking powder and bicarbonate of soda into a bowl.
Stir in the polenta, sugar and blueberries and mix thoroughly.

Mix the yogurt, lemon juice and grated zest, corn oil and crushed
pineapple in another bowl. Pour the liquid into the dry ingredients and briefly stir in.

Add just enough apple juice to make the batter soft and easy to
spoon into the moulds. Spoon the mixture evenly between the
holes in the baking tray and bake for about 20 minutes, or until
golden brown.

Leave in the tray for 5 minutes and then transfer to a wire rack
to cool completely.

SCONES

Serves 6

INGREDIENTS
100g/4oz barley flour, plus extra for dusting
100g/4oz rice flour
1/2 tsp salt
2 tsp gluten-free baking powder
1 tbsp caster sugar
50g/2oz butter, cubed
1 large egg, beaten
5 tbsp milk, plus extra to glaze

Preheat the oven to 230°C/450°F/Gas mark 8.

Sift the flours, salt, baking powder and sugar into a large bowl
and rub in the butter until the mixture resembles breadcrumbs.
Make a well in the centre of the dry ingredients and stir in the
egg and milk to make a soft dough.

Turn the dough out on to a floured surface and knead quickly
and lightly. Gently flatten the dough with the palm of your hand
until it is about 2cm/3/4in thick. Using a floured 5cm/2in cutter,
cut out as many rounds as you can.

Carefully place all the rounds on the hot baking tray and brush
them with a little extra milk. Bake in the oven for about 8 to 10
minutes, or until they are firm. Cool the scones on a wire rack
before serving.

CHRISTMAS CAKE

Serves 8

INGREDIENTS

175g/6oz dried dates, chopped into small pieces
150ml/¹/₄pt water
125ml/4fl oz sunflower oil
25g/1oz ground almonds
1 tsp mixed spice
3 eggs
50g/2oz soya flour
50g/2oz fine maize flour
50g/2oz rice flour
450g/1lb mixed dried fruit

Preheat the oven to 170°C/330°F/Gas mark 3. Grease a 20cm/8in cake tin with butter and line with greaseproof paper.

Place the dates in a pan with the water over a high heat. Bring to the boil and simmer over a low heat for approximately 10 minutes until the dates are soft, then leave to cool.

Beat together the dates, oil, ground almonds, spices, eggs and flours until they are well blended. Stir in the dried fruit and mix well.

Place in the prepared cake tin and bake in the oven for 30 minutes, then lower the temperature to 145°C/290°F/Gas mark 1 for a further 45 minutes.

WALNUT SYRUP CAKE

Serves 10

INGREDIENTS

75g/3oz butter, plus extra for greasing
150g/5oz granulated sugar
4 eggs
150g/5oz rice flour
3 tsp gluten-free baking powder
Pinch of salt
1 tsp cinnamon
75ml/3fl oz milk
1 tsp vanilla essence
150g/5oz chopped walnuts

For the syrup:
100g/4oz granulated sugar
1 cinnamon stick
250ml/9fl oz water
1 tbsp orange juice

Preheat the oven to 180°C/350°F/Gas mark 4. Grease a 20cm/8in cake tin with butter.

Cream the butter and sugar and continue beating until fluffy. Add the eggs to the mixture slowly and continue beating until light.

Stir together the rice flour, baking powder, salt and cinnamon, then add alternately to the butter mixture with the milk. Add the vanilla essence and beat until smooth. Fold in the walnuts. Pour into the prepared cake tin and bake for 30 minutes or until a skewer inserted in the centre comes out clean.

Combine the syrup ingredients in a saucepan and bring to the boil over a medium heat, stirring constantly to dissolve the sugar and boil 10 minutes without stirring. Leave to cool for 5 minutes. Remove the cake from the oven and score the top. Pour the syrup over the cake and leave to stand for several hours.

BANANA SPONGE CAKE

Serves 10

INGREDIENTS
15g/¹/₂oz butter, plus extra for greasing
¹/₂ large banana
1 large egg
50g/2oz granulated sugar
50g/2oz cornflour
25g/1oz potato flour
¹/₂ tsp bicarbonate of soda
¹/₄ tsp cream of tartar
¹/₄ tsp tartaric acid

Preheat the oven to 160°C/325°F/Gas mark 3. Grease a 20cm/8in cake tin with butter and line with greaseproof paper.

In a blender or food processor, blend the banana to a smooth purée with the egg.

Cream the butter and the sugar together in a bowl.

In a separate bowl, sieve together the flours, bicarbonate of soda, cream of tartar and tartaric acid.

Beat the banana mixture gradually into the butter and sugar by hand. Fold in the flour and place the mixture in the prepared cake tin.

Bake in the oven for 20 to 30 minutes, until golden brown. Stand for 10 minutes before turning out on to a wire rack to cool.

VIENNESE CHOCOLATE CAKE

Serves 8

INGREDIENTS

175g/6oz butter, plus extra for greasing
300g/11oz dark chocolate, broken into small pieces
100g/4oz caster sugar
4 eggs, separated
50g/2oz gluten-free breadcrumbs
100g/4oz ground almonds
2 tbsp sugar-free raspberry jam
50g/2oz icing sugar
2 tbsp black coffee

Preheat the oven to 180°C/350°F/Gas mark 4. Grease a 23cm/9in loose-bottomed cake tin with butter and line with greaseproof paper.

Place half the chocolate in a bowl and melt over a pan of simmering water. Cream 100g/4oz butter and the caster sugar together in a bowl. Stir in the egg yolks, breadcrumbs and almonds, then fold in the chocolate and beat well.

In a separate clean bowl, whisk the egg whites until stiff and then fold half at a time into the chocolate mixture. Pour into the prepared cake tin. Bake in the oven for 40 minutes until firm to the touch. Allow to cool for 45 minutes and then brush the cake with the jam.

Melt the remaining chocolate and butter together in a bowl over simmering water. Sift in the icing sugar and beat in the coffee, then leave to stand for 5 minutes. Spread the icing all over the cake and serve chilled.

ORANGE AND APRICOT MUFFINS

Serves 8

INGREDIENTS
50g/2oz butter, melted, plus extra for greasing
75g/3oz rice flour
100g/4oz gluten-free cornmeal
1 tbsp gluten-free baking powder
Pinch of salt
50g/2oz soft brown sugar
200ml/7fl oz milk
1 egg, beaten
Grated zest of 1 orange
150g/5oz ready-to-eat dried apricots, chopped

Preheat the oven to 200°C/400°F/Gas mark 6. Lightly grease 8 deep muffin tins with butter.

Place the flour, cornmeal, baking powder and salt in a bowl and mix.

Stir together the butter, sugar, milk, egg and orange zest, then pour the mixture over the dry ingredients. Fold the ingredients gently together so that they are combined but the mixture is still lumpy.

Fold in the apricots, then spoon the mixture equally between the prepared muffin tins.

Bake in the oven for 15 to 20 minutes until the muffins have risen and are golden brown. Turn them out on to a wire rack to cool.

BREADS

Before you were told you were gluten intolerant, you probably didn't give bread much thought. However, now you've been told you can't eat it, you may realise what a large portion of meals this affects, from a roll with your soup, to a sandwich, and even many deep-fried foods are coated in breadcrumbs. Gluten-free bread in the supermarkets can be expensive and a little bland, so here are some breads that are gluten-free but rich in flavour. Pancakes, cornbread and crispbreads – there is more of a range here than you would probably have tried if you were not gluten-intolerant!

EGG BREAD

Makes one 450g/1lb loaf

INGREDIENTS
50g/2oz potato flour
75g/3oz rice flour
75g/3oz cornflour
1 tsp bicarbonate of soda
1/4 tsp tartaric acid
1/2 tsp cream of tartar
Pinch of salt
1 tsp caster sugar
1 tbsp olive oil
2 eggs, beaten
150ml/1/4pt milk

Preheat the oven to 220°C/425°F/Gas mark 7. Line a shallow 25cm/10in baking tin with greaseproof paper.

In a large mixing bowl combine the flours, bicarbonate of soda, tartaric acid, cream of tartar, salt and sugar with the oil.

Beat the milk and egg together, then fold the flour mixture into the beaten egg.

Place the mixture into the prepared baking tin and bake in the oven for 40 to 45 minutes, until an inserted skewer comes out clean. Turn out on to a wire tray to cool.

CRANBERRY BREAD

Serves 10

INGREDIENTS
25g/1oz butter, plus extra for greasing
200g/7oz rice flour, plus extra for dusting
100g/4oz potato flour
50g/2oz tapioca flour
75g/3oz potato starch
1/2 tsp salt
3 tsp gluten-free baking powder
200g/7oz granulated sugar
200g/7oz dried cranberries
2 eggs, beaten
200ml/7fl oz orange juice

Preheat the oven to 180°C/350°F/Gas mark 4. Grease a loaf tin with butter and dust with rice flour.

Sift together the flours, potato starch, salt, baking powder and sugar. Mix for 2 minutes, then add the cranberries. Add beaten eggs, butter and orange juice and mix well.

Place the batter in the prepared loaf tin and bake in the oven for 45 minutes. Cool on a wire rack before serving.

FRUIT AND SEED BREAD

Makes one 450g/1lb loaf

INGREDIENTS

Butter, for greasing
150g/5oz chickpea flour
150g/5oz gluten-free flour
2 tsp easy-blend dried yeast
1 tsp caster sugar
1 tsp salt
1 tbsp black onion seeds
1 tbsp cumin seeds
1/4 tsp dried chilli flakes
2 tsp ground coriander
50g/2oz dried pear, chopped
2 tbsp refined groundnut oil
200ml/7fl oz hand-hot water

Grease a 450g/1lb loaf tin with butter.

Put the flours, yeast, sugar, salt, black onion seeds, cumin seeds, chilli flakes, coriander and pear in a bowl and mix together.

Add the oil and water and mix to a stiff paste.

Turn into the prepared loaf tin, cover loosely with oiled clingfilm and leave in a warm place for about 45 minutes until the mixture rises slightly above the top of the tin. Preheat the oven to 200°C/400°F/Gas mark 6. Remove the clingfilm.

Bake in the oven for 25 minutes or until firm to the touch. Turn out on to a wire rack to cool.

CARROT FLAT BREAD

Makes one 450g/1lb loaf

INGREDIENTS
Butter, for greasing
100g/4oz carrot, grated
150ml/^{1}/$_4$pt milk
1 egg
25g/1oz olive oil
75g/3oz cornflour
100g/4oz rice flour
25g/1oz powdered milk
1 tsp bicarbonate of soda
^{1}/$_3$ tsp cream of tartar
^{1}/$_4$ tsp tartaric acid
1 tsp granulated sugar
^{1}/$_2$ tsp salt

Preheat the oven to 220°C/425°F/Gas mark 7. Grease a 450g/1lb loaf tin with butter and line with greaseproof paper.

In a blender or food processor, beat the carrot to a smooth purée with the milk and egg.

Mix together the oil, flours, powdered milk, bicarbonate of soda, cream of tartar, tartaric acid, sugar and salt. Fold the flour mixture into the purée, being careful not to over mix.

Spread the mixture in the prepared loaf tin and bake in the oven for 35 to 45 minutes. Check it is cooked by inserting a skewer. The loaf is not cooked until the skewer comes out clean. Serve immediately.

PIZZA CRUST

Makes one 30cm/12in pizza

INGREDIENTS

1 tbsp gluten-free dry yeast
175g/6oz brown rice flour, plus extra for dusting
100g/4oz tapioca flour
2 tbsp powdered milk
2 tsp xanthan gum
$1/2$ tsp salt
1 tsp gelatine powder
200ml/7fl oz warm water
$1/4$ tsp clear honey
1 tsp olive oil
1 tsp cider vinegar

Preheat the oven to 200°C/400°F/Gas mark 6.

In medium bowl, beat together the yeast, flours, powdered milk, xanthan gum, salt and gelatine powder. Add the water, honey, olive oil, and vinegar. Beat well for three minutes, adding more water if necessary.

Put the mixture into 30cm/12in pizza pan. Liberally sprinkle rice flour on to the dough, then press dough into pan, continuing to sprinkle dough with flour to prevent sticking to your hands.

Bake the pizza crust for 10 minutes. Remove from the oven and spread with the sauce and toppings of your choice. Bake for a further 20 to 25 minutes or until nicely browned.

BREAKFAST CORNBREAD

Makes 8 slices

INGREDIENTS
25g/1oz butter, melted, plus extra for greasing
100g/4oz gluten-free cornmeal
75g/3oz chickpea flour
1 1/2 tsp gluten-free baking powder
Salt and pepper
1 egg
250ml/9fl oz milk

Preheat the oven to 170°C/325°F/Gas mark 3. Lightly grease a
450g/1lb loaf tin with butter.

Put the cornmeal, flour, baking powder and a little salt and
pepper in a bowl and make a well in the centre. Beat the egg
with the milk and butter and add a little to the bowl.

Beat with a whisk, gradually incorporating the dry ingredients to
make a smooth paste. Add the remaining milk mixture and whisk
until smooth.

Turn into the prepared tin and bake in the oven for 25 to 30
minutes until just firm. Leave in the tin for 10 minutes, then
transfer to a wire rack to cool.

BUTTERMILK PANCAKES

Serves 5

INGREDIENTS
300g/11oz white rice flour
100g/4oz tapioca flour
50g/2oz potato starch flour
150g/5oz buttermilk powder
1 tbsp granulated sugar
1 tsp gluten-free baking powder
1/2 tsp salt
2 eggs
250ml/9fl oz water
2 tbsp vegetable oil, plus extra for frying

Sift the flours, buttermilk powder, sugar, baking powder and salt together into a mixing bowl.

Beat the eggs with the water and oil, and add to the dry ingredients. Beat together until the batter is smooth, but do not over beat.

Drop from the mixing spoon on to a hot frying pan with oil and cook until the top is full of tiny bubbles and the underside is brown. Turn and brown the other side, then serve hot.

CHESTNUT CRISPBREAD

Makes 15 crispbreads

INGREDIENTS
Butter, for greasing
100g/4oz sunflower seeds
100g/4oz sweet chestnut purée
50g/2oz sorghum flour
25g/1oz lard, melted

Preheat the oven to 200°C/400°F/Gas mark 6. Lightly grease a baking tray with butter.

In a blender or food processor, liquidize the sunflower seeds with the sweet chestnut purée. Then mix in the flour and lard.

Take a walnut-sized lump of dough and place it between two sheets of greaseproof paper. Roll it until it is 5mm/¼in thick. Peel off the paper and place the crispbreads on the prepared baking tray.

Bake in the oven for 10 minutes, or until golden brown, then turn out on to a wire tray to cool.

RICE BREAD

Makes one 450g/1lb loaf

INGREDIENTS
1 large banana, chopped
1 egg
150ml/¼pt milk
100g/4oz rice flour
100g/4oz potato flour
1 tsp bicarbonate of soda
½ tsp cream of tartar
¼ tsp tartaric acid
Pinch of salt
1 tsp caster sugar
1 tbsp olive oil

Preheat the oven to 220°C/425°F/Gas mark 7. Line a 25cm/10in shallow square baking tin with greaseproof paper.

In a blender or food processor, beat the banana to a smooth purée with the milk and egg.

In a large mixing bowl, combine the flours, bicarbonate of soda, cream of tartar, tartaric acid, salt and sugar with the oil. Fold the flour mixture into the purée.

Pour the batter, 2.5cm/1in deep, into the prepared baking tin lined with non-stick baking parchment.

Bake in the oven for 35 to 45 minutes, until an inserted skewer comes out clean.

BANANA BREAD
Makes 18 slices

INGREDIENTS
75g/3oz butter, plus extra for greasing
200g/7oz rice flour
150g/5oz potato starch flour
3 tsp gluten-free baking powder
1/4 tsp salt
1 tbsp unflavoured gelatine powder
100g/4oz granulated sugar
3 egg yolks
1 tsp vanilla essence
1 tsp grated lemon zest
4 bananas, mashed
150ml/1/4pt plain yogurt
3 egg whites

Preheat the oven to 180°C/350°F/Gas mark 4. Grease a loaf pan with butter.

Sift the flours, baking powder, salt and gelatine together.

Cream the butter, sugar, egg yolks and vanilla essence thoroughly. Continue beating until the mixture is light. Mix in the lemon zest, banana and yoghurt, the add the flour mixture.

In a separate bowl beat the egg whites to stiff peaks, then fold into the mixture. Place in the greased loaf pan and bake in the oven for 1 hour.

Weights and Measures

Imperial	Metric	Imperial	Metric
1oz	25g	1³/₄lb	850g
2oz	50g	2lb	900g
3oz	75g	2¹/₂lb	1.1kg
4oz	100g	3lb	1.4kg
5oz	150g	3¹/₂lb	1.6kg
6oz	175g	4lb	1.8kg
7oz	200g	4¹/₂lb	2kg
8oz	225g	5lb	2.3kg
9oz	250g	5¹/₂lb	2.5kg
10oz	275g	6lb	2.7kg
11oz	300g	6¹/₂lb	3kg
12oz	350g	7lb	3.2kg
13oz	375g	7¹/₂lb	3.4kg
14oz	400g	8lb	3.6kg
15oz	425g	8¹/₂lb	3.9kg
16oz (1lb)	450g	9lb	4.1kg
1lb 2oz	500g	9¹/₂lb	4.3kg
1¹/₄lb	600g	10lb	4.5kg
1¹/₂lb	700g		

Imperial	Metric	Imperial	Metric
1fl oz	25ml	9fl oz	250ml
2fl oz	50ml	10fl oz (¹/₂pt)	300ml
3fl oz	75ml	12fl oz	350ml
3¹/₂fl oz	100ml	15fl oz (³/₄pt)	450ml
4fl oz	125ml	18 fl oz	500ml
5fl oz (¹/₄pt)	150ml	20fl oz (1pt)	600ml
6fl oz	175ml	30fl oz (1¹/₂pt)	900ml
7fl oz	200ml	35 fl oz (2pt)	1.2 litres
8fl oz	225ml	40 fl oz (2¹/₂pt)	1.5 litres

All the measurements given are for level spoonfuls (British Imperial Standard). 1 teaspoon = 5ml, 1 tablespoon = 15ml